101 Dartmoor Letterboxes

but not how to find them

by

JOHN HAYWARD

with Anne Swinscow

KIRKFORD PUBLICATIONS

First Published March 1988
Reprinted 1992, 1995.
By Kirkford Publications
Cross Farm, Diptford, Totnes, Devon

Other books on letterboxing by Anne Swinscow

Dartmoor Letterboxes
More Dartmoor Letterboxes

ISBN 0 9509114 3 7

Typeset by Exe Valley Dataset, Exeter
Printed and bound by BPC Wheatons Ltd, Exeter

There is something special about letterboxing that tends to bring out a crazy streak in everyone. The idea of retired businessmen rushing about Dartmoor looking for a rubber stamp depicting Paddington Bear may seem quaint to the uninitiated, but it beats watching T.V. on a Sunday afternoon any day!

The serious walker, or the average stroller and his family, can get equal pleasure from boxhunting, and nearly all who start letterboxing become addicted.

You have been warned . . .

Introduction

by Anne Swinscow

Just in case anyone doesn't know what a Dartmoor letterbox is, I will explain that it is a cache, usually an ammunition tin or similar receptacle that is hidden on the moor. Inside is a rubber stamp, an inkpad, and a visitors' book. The object of letterboxing is to collect impressions of the stamps and sign the visitors' books, proving that you have been there.

Some years ago, as an added incentive to boxhunters, my husband Godfrey started the "100 Club". He has since been described as "the unofficial president of a non-existent club", an apt way of putting it as there are no club premises, no subscription, and no official meetings. The only essential for membership is that one must have visited 100 different Dartmoor letterboxes.

When people achieve this goal they usually send in a list of the boxes they have found and—on payment of 70p—receive a cloth badge. John Hayward went one better: he sent not only the stamps he had collected, but also 100 sketches showing the locality where each one was found. From that original idea he and I have produced this book.

Dartmoor is a wonderful place, and what better way to enjoy its beauties than to walk over it on letterbox hunts? Many of the boxes have a story attached: folklore, legends, industrial archaeology, flora, and fauna are all to be found on the stamps. The ones we have used for this book are not necessarily in John's original 100, nor are they chosen because they are the best on the Moor. There are many others just as good, but we felt that these provided a representative selection. Though John has written in the present tense this does NOT mean that these boxes are all still there. Boxes come and go; these were collected over the course of a year.

Because each box belongs to someone it is private property; we therefore give no clues to finding them. The owners may reveal their whereabouts to whom they wish. Five boxes are shown on the Ordnance Survey maps, and these should give anyone new to the game a start.

There are two other types of letterboxes which are now very popular, pub boxes and "travellers". A great many of the pubs within the National Park now have a stamp and visitors' book behind the bar, and while this is no doubt good for trade it also provides letterboxers with an excellent excuse for a break. A "traveller" is a box that is carried about on the Moor by a letterboxer: this is different from a "personal stamp" which many boxers use instead of a signature in the visitors' books. Though "pub boxes" and "travellers" are not true letterboxes in the sense that they will qualify one for membership of the "100 Club", they form an excellent way of meeting other boxers, and are an enjoyable off-shoot of the original concept.

Some years ago a box was put out where everyone who signed in was asked to write a poem in the book. Since that time poems and letterboxing seem to have gone hand in hand, and letterboxers break into verse at the slightest provocation. To help you on your way as you tramp over the moors John has written some jolly marching songs, all to rhythms that we hope will be familiar. This too may become habit forming, so when you tire of the ones he has written have a go yourself. But don't get so engrossed that you forget to look about you: there is a lot to enjoy on Dartmoor and a lot to learn, and we hope that letterboxing will encourage you to do both to the full.

But remember:

Every box belongs to someone, and it is the owner's responsibility to see that it is well sited, and does not give offence to the landowner, nor interfere with any of the antiquities on the Moor. For this reason a "Code of Conduct" has been produced, which states . . .

Boxes should not be sited:
1. In any kind of Antiquity,
     in or near Stone Rows, Circles, Cists or Cairns,
     in any kind of building, wall or ruin.
2. In any potentially dangerous situation
     where injuries could be sustained.
3. As a fixture. Cement or any other
     building material may not be used.

Letterboxers should follow the Country Code.

The same rules must apply to those who hunt for boxes, and I would stress that though some of the stamps may represent ruins or antiquities, the box will be found some way away. So PLEASE, PLEASE never disturb any of Dartmoor's historical remains.

We hope that this book will not only help add to the fun of letterboxing, but will help you appreciate some of the natural beauties and history of Dartmoor.

GOOD HUNTING

LITTLE BOXES

Once upon a time there were three little foxes, but . . .

Out on the Moor there are hundreds of boxes,
Pushed out of sight under boulders and rockses.
They were put there by walkers with very long legses,
Who always wear big boots and two pairs of sockses.

They like it much better than being in shopses,
Jostled by customers, robbers, and copses;
For here they can talk to the beetles and wormses,
And have a singsong with the crickets and wopses.

They stay in the darkness until the sun rises,
Waiting for visitors, galses and guyses,
Who often arrive wet through to their skinses
Having sunk in a bog right up to their thighses.

They pass all their lives in neat little houses:
They often have friends but never have spouses.
On Sat'days and Sundays they listen for voices,
But on weekdays they gossip with rabbits and mouses.

They're never molested by badgers or foxes,
So please treat them likewise, you searchers for boxes,
Youngsters and oldsters and boyses and girlses
In wellies and trainers and trousies and frockses.

4

Hay Tor   *Saddle Tor*

Before the cattle grid was set into the road there was an old gate here whose mighty granite posts now lie sleeping in the grass beside the highway. There is, almost within a stone's throw, a wall, a manorial bound stone, a Bronze Age cairn, a burial chamber, a vanished inn, and prehistoric fields; and on the nearby tor, a stone cross, some abandoned millstones, and three huge cairns; and from the summit, one of the most magnificent views to be found anywhere along the borders of the Moor.

Truly this is a Gateway to Dartmoor, and the letterbox, which looks down on the gate, will provide the finder with an appropriate stamp to start a collection.

THE WAY TO CRANMERE

A tourist at Meldon approaches a well-laden, weather-beaten walker
whose rucksack bears a "1000 letterbox" badge.

With memories of C. G. Rossetti

How far is it to Cranmere on the Moor?
   Seven miles there and six miles back.
Do many people go there to explore?
   Yes, and most come back.

     Could I walk to Cranmere, do you think?
        You have two legs, I see.
     And when I get there is there food and drink?
        In your rucksack it will be.

          Does the route go uphill all the way?
             Except for fifteen yards or so.
          And shall I get both there and back today?
             That depends how fast you go.

               I've heard that mires cover half the land.
                  Of that there is no doubt.
               If I fall in would there be help at hand?
                  There's none to hear you shout.

                    What signs are there to guide me on my way?
                      Take a map and compass, friend.
                    But in the mist I might well go astray?
                      Then if you don't come back 'twill be the end.

CRANMERE

CRANE'S MERE

On Dartmoor the Heron used to be called the Crane.

This is where it all began, in 1854. In that year James Perrott of Chagford placed a bottle in a bank here as a receptacle for visitors' cards. Later a box was substituted and a book added. The present concrete and iron box is the largest and most obvious on the Moor— but in misty weather you'll need a map, a compass, and some experience to find it.

There is still a pool at Cranmere, in a little hollow that Benjamin Gayer, Mayor of Okehampton, must have missed. For according to legend he was condemned for sheep stealing and sentenced to empty the mere with a sieve. This he achieved by wrapping his sieve in a piece of skin from a handy dead sheep. There are of course more prosaic stories to explain how the mere was drained, but since the Spirit of Benjie still haunts the area, the old story is more acceptable.

GEAR'S SIEVE

To be sung to the tune of "Drake's Drum"

In memory of Benjie Gear, Mayor of Okehampton

Gear he stole a sheep or two not half a mile away,
  (Benjie, art tha list'nin there below?)
Was sentenced by the magistrate when came his judgment day
  To cleanin' out the pool at Cranmere-O.
They took him up the Okement, made sure he reached the place,
  An, left him there to talk to crane an' crow.
"Now don't yu start a-wailin'. Just get busy bailin'."
  They gave to him a sieve, and left in half a mo'.

Gear he then got busy and plied his little sieve.
  (Benjie, art tha list'nin there below?)
'Twern't much use at all, but it's all that he was giv'
  For dippin' with to empty Cranmere-O.
"Bain't no gude t'me", says he, "I'll niver git it done.
  Must look around for somethin' else for sure, I know."
Just then a sheep appearin', old Ben approached it, leerin',
  An' the poor thing took afright, an' died in half a mo'.

Gear he then made use o' what the sheep could give,
  (Benjie, art tha list'nin there below?)
Cut a piece o' sheepskin to wrap around his sieve
  For bailin' out the pool at Cranmere-O.
Knelt down on the soggy peat, bent upon his task:
  Dip an' lift, fetch an' carry, to an' fro,
His arm kept swingin', but now his heart was singin'
  As he emptied out the pool in half a mo'.

CUCKOOS

Dartmoor has an abundance of CUCKOOS. Apart from those that fly there is near Western Beacon a rounded hill called Cuckoo Ball; near Buttern Hill stands Cuckoo Stone; and here on the Western slopes of Combshead Tor is the well-known Cuckoo Rock. Here also is one of the longer established letterboxes. The first one was placed on top of the rock, but in true cuckoo style its present offspring may be found in another nest.

Beneath the rock is a small cave which is one of a number on the Moor said to have been once used to store smuggled brandy.

*Longaford Tor
on the Southeast horizon*

Crows and Rooks are both common on the moor. The old way of distinguishing them still holds good: "If you can see lots of Crows they are Rooks, but if the Rook is all by itself it's a Crow."

When you have found the letterbox—which is easy-climb up to the platform and find Golden Rod, Bluebell, Whortleberry, Great Woodrush, and Wavy Hairgrass.

Golden Rod

The Devil's Kitchen

Here is one of Dartmoor's wildest and most beautiful cleaves.

Two letterboxes are sited within sound of the rushing waters, but even if you can't find them the walk will have been rewarding.

Here along the road from Cherry Brook to East Dart is the Happy Hunting Ground of the Hairy Hands.
Who will be next to experience his hirsute hold?

A short walk and a long search may reveal his hiding place.

Many of the stories of accidents along this stretch of road date from the 1920s. On three separate occasions a motor-cyclist was forced on to the verge. One of them was killed; the other two both spoke of powerful hands gripping the handlebars. A coach driver whose vehicle mounted the bank mentioned the same phenomenon, and a caravanner not far away described hairy hands clawing at the window during the night. One walker along the road heard screaming beyond the wall, and another in the plantations was overcome by inexplicable panic.

The only recent mystery connected with this road is of a car that overturned one evening—but the driver was killed and could offer no explanation!

THE HAIRY HANDS

Advice to Girl Guides

On Dartmoor it may not be smugglers riding through the night . . .

If you wake at midnight
                    when camping on the Moor,
And hear a snuffling sound
                    that's just beyond the door,
Don't go peeping out
                    to find out what and why:
Just stay inside, m' darling,
                    while the Hairy Hands go by!

> Long and hairy fingers
> Probing through the night,
> Seeking flesh to grapple,
> —Searching left and right—
> Feeling for a handhold
> On a maiden's thigh.

So stay inside, m' darlin',
                    while the Hairy Hands go by!

Don't creep out to arm yourself
                    with saucepan or a stick;
If you left the tentflap open
                    make haste to close it quick!
Wait inside, in terror,
                    till the snuffles die away:
Sleep then—if you can—
                    until the coming of the day.

> Long and hairy fingers
> Probing through the night,
> Seeking flesh to grapple,
> —Searching left and right—
> Feeling for a handhold
> On a maiden's thigh.

Don't give way to panic;
                    don't even bat an eye:
Just stay inside, m' darlin',
                    while the Hairy Hands go by!

13

Here are two of the most pains-taking of Dartmoor writers.

Crossing's "Guide", although written in 1912, has never been bettered. It is still available and is widely used and quoted from by keen Moor walkers. The stamp was made from a photograph taken in 1921 when Crossing was about 73 years old.

In addition to the well-known "Guide" many other books by Crossing make informative and pleasant reading. Tors, moors, rivers, workers, pixies, all are described, and some delightful near-fiction is often included.

Hansford Worth's "Dartmoor", which is also still in print, is too bulky a volume to carry in one's rucksack, but its possession is a 'must' for keen explorers. The work has been described as "a king-pin of Dartmoor literature": it deals with the geography, natural history, and above all the archaeology of the Moor. It is crammed with detailed information and measurements.

A practised eye will find these two boxes without difficulty, but no clue is here given as to their whereabouts, except that they may both be encountered in an hour's walk.

14

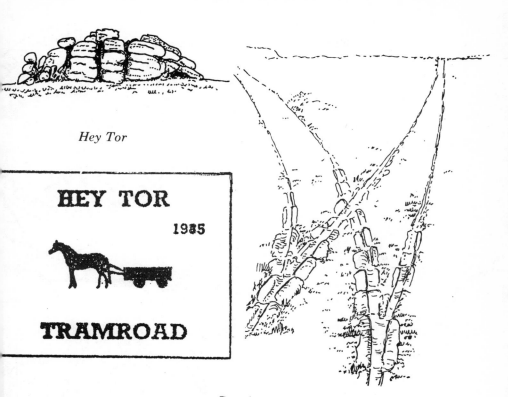

Hey Tor

HEY TOR
1985

TRAMROAD

Granite tramroad

This unusual railway was opened in 1820 to transport granite from the quarries near Hey Tor and Holwell Tor to the canal at Teigngrace, some nine miles away and 1300 feet lower in altitude. The granite rails stood up well to wear and tear, and were far cheaper to lay than iron ones. The quarries were worked on and off during the 19th century, but the railway was little used after about 1860.

The first stretch of line from Holwell quarry runs uphill, and it is said that teams of up to 19 horses were used to pull 12 trucks, laden, all told, with perhaps 30 tons of granite. From the brow of Hey Tor Down most of the rest of the way was downhill. Stone for London Bridge (now in Arizona) and The British Museum came this way.

The letterbox too was probably carried this way (though not in a truck) right to the end of the line.

CHAW is a Dartmoor word for Jack-daw, and these birds once nested in the very deep mining gully of this name which runs along the South-western foot of Birch Tor.

GUARDIAN of CHAW GULL
LEGEND of DARTMOOR

The story goes that in one of the vertical shafts lies a treasure of gold, but those who have attempted to lower themselves down have never climbed back. The raven on guard above gives a croak, a hand comes out of the shaft wall and cuts the rope. The adventurer plunges to a sudden end.

EDGAR ALLAN POE VISITS CHAW GULLY

Another Raven legend

Once upon a Winter Friday when I started out to tidy
Dusty shelves containing ancient volumes of Westcountry lore,
While I nodded, gently browsing, almost to the point of drowsing,
Suddenly a legend, rousing thoughts of gold galore,
Told of treasure long abandoned 'neath a gully near Birch Tor.
    —Dreams of wealth for evermore.

Sleepily I sat there thinking, and my thoughts were busy linking
Tales of tin and gold dug out and hoarded in the days of yore.
Avidly I read the story, learned the details *con anore*,
Revelled in the golden glory that was lying 'neath a tor,
Vowed, with dreams of endless wealth, I would not leave the golden store
    Lying there for evermore.

On the morrow in the morning, taking care to give no warning,
Stealthily I picked my way with torch and rope across the moor.
Eastward now the sky was glowing, but although the day was growing,
Night still filled the gully, throwing shadows on its rocky floor.
Shades to hide a plunge into an unseen pit along the floor—
    To be lost for evermore.

Boldly now my passage wending to the venture fast impending,
Soon I reached the ragged shaft that opened like a gaping door,
When a coal-black raven fluttered to a beetling crag and muttered,
As it were, a warning, uttered croaking hoarsely, to deplore
Such violation of his golden secret 'neath the moor,
    He thought was his for evermore.

But neither threat nor pleading would have swayed me into heeding
Word or sign that menaced my intention to explore.
Down the gully mists were swirling, writhing round the rope unfurling,
Well belayed, then thrown uncurling, down for fifty feet or more.
Quickly then I slithered down, and as I touched the stony floor
    The raven croaked once more.

Torch in hand I paused there standing, when the thud of something landing
Just behind me made me turn and throw the beam across the floor,
Till the dull light dimly streaming found a skull whose mouth was screaming,
And whose eyes were faintly gleaming on my rope upon the floor—
Fifty feet of rope that I would madly grasp from off the floor—
    In my hands for evermore.

Sluice gate above the aqueduct

The miners' spoil-heaps beyond the aqueduct are a favourite haunt of Wheatears.

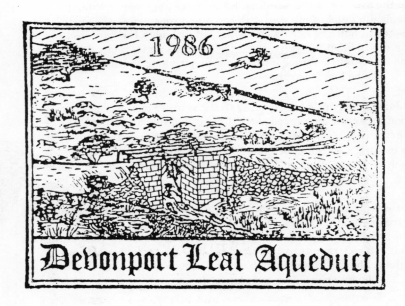

1986

Devonport Leat Aqueduct

The Devonport Leat here crosses the River Meavy by an aqueduct sometimes called the Iron Bridge. After rushing down Raddick Hill, under the sluice and across the Meavy, it continues more soberly down the valley to empty its water into Burrator Reservoir.

END OF RAINBOW

RAINBOWS

Rainbows must have been a source of wonder to mankind ever since he has been able to wonder. On the rare occasions when we can see where a rainbow ends surely we all pause awhile and gaze.

Here are two stamps, prompted by different emotions and placed in letterboxes for different reasons, which express the joy that a rainbow can bring.

Rainbows of course appear and disappear, but if one day you see one in the neighbourhood of Hay Tor then you have a clue to the whereabouts of these two letterboxes: they could well be at opposite ends of that rainbow—and you won't have a long walk.

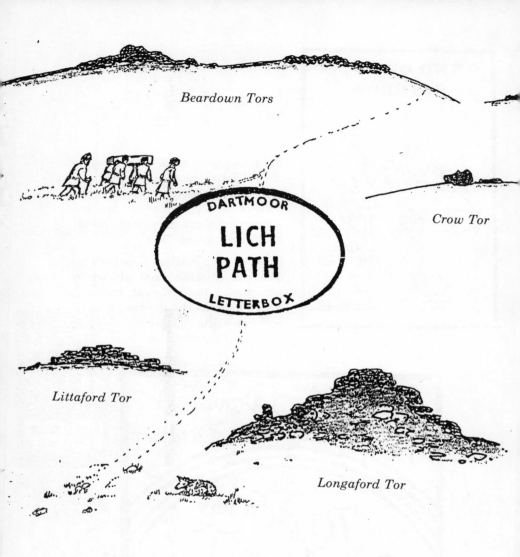

Beardown Tors

Crow Tor

DARTMOOR
**LICH
PATH**
LETTERBOX

Littaford Tor

Longaford Tor

Before about the middle of the 13th Century the bodies of those who died on a large part of Dartmoor had to be carried to Lydford for burial. From settlements such as Bellever this would mean an exhausting journey of perhaps 12 miles along a route now known as the Lich Path or Lych Way. Mists and rivers in spate might lengthen the journey even more, for besides the high moorland the Dart, Cowsic, Walkham, and Tavy had all to be crossed.

At one point along the way mourners—or indeed letterboxers— would be in sight of all these tors.

Steeperton Tor

This is one of Dartmoor's smallest and most remote tin mines. Situated along the banks of the Taw below Steeperton Tor it enjoyed a brief heyday between 1875 and 1878, employing up to about 25 workers. In the latter year production was just one ton of black tin.

The tinners' heaps are easy to find, but remains of the mine house, leat, bridge, and of course the letterbox, are more difficult.

Location of the STRONG BOX will involve some healthy exercise.

STEEPERTON
TIN MINE
1875-1882

*Ford across
the Taw
near Knack Mine*

21

Round-leaved Crowfoot

HORSE FORD on the O Brook was probably once a well used river crossing. It lay on the old monastic East-West route across the Moor that is marked along much of its way by a series of crosses. Holne Moor on one side and Down Ridge on the other each have a cross (and also a letterbox). The original track is now hardly visible, but navigation in clear weather is straightforward—that is, if you can find the next cross!

Upstream from here tin mines were active over a long period, so the miners too may well have splashed across this ford.

The sketch is of a shallow pool in the stream, not the ford, for this was obliterated by a surge of boulders during a storm in 1965.

ONE MORE RIVER

The Song of the Ten Letterbox walk

"There's one more river to cross"

Collect ten boxes all today?
  There's one more river to cross.
Then here's your list. Be on your way.
  There's one more river to cross.

CHORUS One more river,
      And that's the river of Ockyment
      There's one more river,
      There's one more river to cross.

One Sunday morn they all set out.
  There's one more river to cross.
When evening came they were quite
  worn out.
  There's one more river to cross

CHORUS

They crossed the Okement one by one,
JUST JAKE by himself, old son of a gun.
  There's one more river to cross.

They crossed the Okement two by two,
Poor SOGGY SOX with one sodden shoe.
  There's one more river to cross.

They crossed the Okement three by
  three,
INTREPID STAMPER with EWE AND ME.
  There's one more river to cross.

They crossed the Okement four by four,
THE TWITCHERS THREE and OTHELLO THE
  MOOR.
  There's one more river to cross.

They crossed the Okement five by five,
THE BOG-COTTON STOMPERS determined
  to arrive.
  There's one more river to cross.

They crossed the Okement six by six,
THE VISI-TORS with MR CHIPS.
  There's one more river to cross.

They crossed the Okement seven by
  seven,
THE DARTMOOR-AUDERS going to Heaven.
  There's one more river to cross.

They crossed the Okement eight by eight,
THE SILLY BOGGER helping KAMIKAZE
  KATE.
  There's one more river to cross.

They crossed the Okement nine by nine,
THE BLOTTS ON THE LANDSCAPE all doing
  fine.
  There's one more river to cross.

They crossed the Okement ten by ten,
Trying to keep up with THE FLOWERPOT
  MEN.
  There's one more river to cross.

CHORUS

From Kitty Tor to High Willee
  There's one more river to cross.

From Fordsland Ledge to Slipp'ry Stones
  There's one more river to cross.

From Great Kneeset to Dingdong Tor
  There's one more river to cross.

From Lints Tor Brook to Jackman's B'm
  There's one more river to cross.

CHORUS

Where else they went I could not say,
  There's one more river to cross.
But sure, they had a busy day.
  There's one more river to cross.

One more river,
  And that's the river of Ockyment,
    There's one more river,
      There's one more river
        to cross.

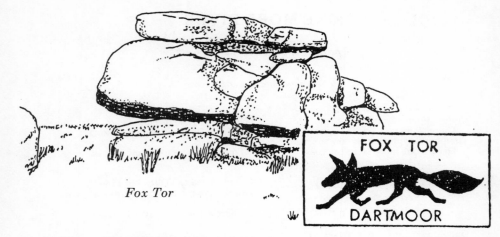

Fox Tor

FOX TOR

DARTMOOR

Foxes abound on the moor. Their dens may be found in the heather, in old mine workings, and among clitter. Although hunted they probably maintain their numbers without difficulty. Rabbits, mice, voles, and beetles form the bulk of their diet. Occasionally eggs or young of ground nesting birds may be taken.

From FOX TOR you can look down and see the cross at Childe's Tomb, one of the "three remarkable things of Dartmoor". If you have forgotten the story the song on the opposite page will remind you.

Fox Tor naturally has a letter-fox. The one at Methern Brook is there because this stream is also called Foxholes Water.

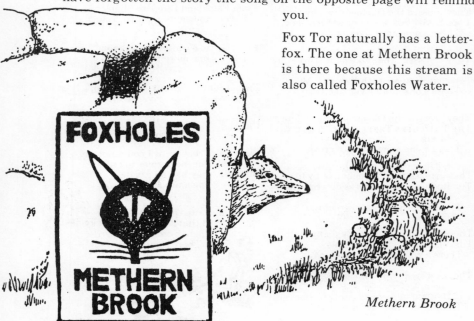

FOXHOLES

METHERN BROOK

Methern Brook

24

CHILDE HAROLD

*To be sung, while struggling through Fox Tor Mire,
to the tune of "My Bonnie lies over the ocean".*

Childe Harold was riding 'cross Dartmoor,
  The snow came right up to his knees,
Childe Harold was lost upon Dartmoor,
  One night when it started to freeze.

CHORUS What did, what did, what did poor Harold do then?
         What did, what did, O what did poor Harold do then?

Childe Harold got down from his
     horse then,
  He'd made up his mind what to
  do.
He unsheathed his sword in a
     twinkling
  And severed its jugular
  through.

CHORUS

He next disembowelled the creature
  To fashion a shelter forlorn;
He snuggled right in to the carcase
  And lay down to wait for the
  morn.

CHORUS

The liver he had for a pillow,
  The rib-cage provided his bed;
But the blizzard blew on to his torso
And froze him until he was dead.

CHORUS

A party of monks found the carcase
  With Harold's stiff body inside,
One thumb was stuck out at an
     angle
  As if he were hitching a ride.

CHORUS

Childe Harold went riding 'cross
     Dartmoor
  Childe Harold crossed over the
  mire.
They carried his corpse to the Abbey
  And thawed it in front of the fire.

What will, what will, what will poor
  Harold do now?
What will, what will, O what will
  poor Harold do now?

These are the only circles on Dartmoor paired in this way. They are also the largest in diameter, though they are not identical. The circles were 'restored' in 1909 when many fallen stones (over half the total) were re-erected.

Part of Fernworthy Plantation

One explanation for so many of the stones' being recumbent is that once upon a time wives suspected of being faithless had to kneel in supplication before one of the stones. If she was inno-

The Grey Wethers

cent nothing happened, but if she was guilty the stone promptly fell on top of her.

Another oft-repeated story tells how the stones were once sold as two flocks of sheep (or wethers). Since the sale took place at the Warren House Inn the vendor had plenty of time to decamp before the buyer could inspect his new flocks here on the slopes of Sittaford Tor. Caveat emptor!

Visitors to the letterbox (which is a little way away) are asked to record the weather at the time of their visit. The records make interesting reading.

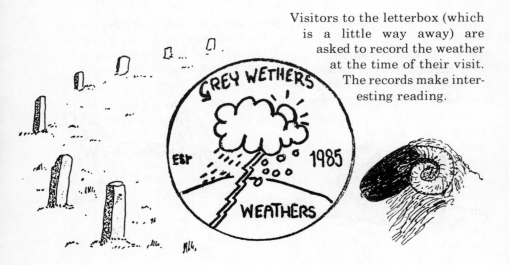

26

*Phillpotts memorial
at North end of
Black Ridge Peat Pass*

The great blanket bog that covers much of Northern Dartmoor is tiring walking country, and for a rider is in places impassable.

Some hundreds of years ago the moormen cut a pass through the bog on the slopes of Cut Hill, which became known as Cut Lane; and at the end of the 19th century a number of others were cut under the direction of Frank Phillpotts. These passes are generally about 3 to 5 feet below surface level and offer firm walking. Finding them however needs either good visibility or good navigation. Most of them have a memorial stone at each end, and where the peat has been further eroded along their course small cairns of whitish stones indicate the proper route. In poor weather these are a godsend and all care should be taken to maintain them. The longest pass runs for nearly a kilometre along Black Ridge, where in the centre an acre or so of peat has disappeared leaving huge hags rising from the pass floor.

Several letterboxes have been associated with these passes. Here is one of the newer ones.

Widecombe

Wittaburrow

LETTERBOXES
FOR
CHILDREN

Postman Pat is on his rounds. He is driving from Widecombe up to Wittaburrow where he has a special box to visit. Later he will deliver a letter addressed to Miss Tor who of course lives on the slopes of Little Mis Tor.

These two boxes should appeal to those children who—willingly or otherwise—accompany their parents on hunting expeditions. One of them is occasionally stocked with Smarties.

Little Mis Tor

TODDLER'S CORNER

SOME DARTMOOR NURSERY RHYMES

Postman, postman, where have you been?
I've been to Vur Tor to visit the Queen.
Postman, postman, how were the rocks?
Too many letters and not enough box.

Hey, diddle, duddle,
The flat-rods and buddle,
The cow jumped over the leat,
The stamping mill laughed to see such sport,
And the dog ran off with the meat.

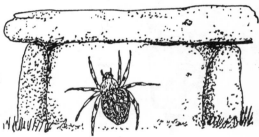

Here's Mary Jane in a cold
    kistvaen,
Her knees tucked up to her head.
Along came a spider, and snuggled
    beside her,
But soon found out she was dead.

Three nice girls, three nice girls,
They all ran after the moorman's son,
So every day when his work was done
He took them all out and had lots of fun
With three nice girls.

Western Beacon.

*Cairn and
Parish boundary stone*

This is the southernmost height within the National Park, and the view from here on a clear day extends across the South Hams to the English Channel. It is called Western Beacon to distinguish it from Easte n Beacon, which lies on Ugborough Down about a mile to the Northeast.

The stamp in this letterbox is a prized one as the three parts of it may be printed in three colours to make a design in 'glorious technicolor'.

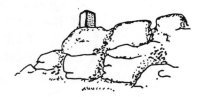

Easdon Tor

Not all letterboxes are associated with places of historical or topographical interest. Some are put out just for the pleasure that others may have in finding them.

Here are two stamps to illustrate the satisfaction of their discoverers, one quiet, the other exuberant. The first has climbed an outlying tor, the second has perhaps crossed boggy ground to find a babbling brook where the afternoon sunshine warms a high bank.

Blackaton Brook

The satisfaction of reaching Fur Tor is not surpassed at any other place on the Moor. It is one of the grandest and certainly the most remote tor on Dartmoor. 'Fur' is probably a corruption of either the Celtic 'Vwr' (Great) or the Saxon 'Feor' (Far). 'Vur Tor' its local pronunciation would perhaps be a better spelling.

This is one of the older letterboxes, now maintained by the Park Rangers. There is no secret about its hiding place.

Here are some of the stamps found there over the years

IN DARTYMOOR FOREST

Remembered from when we were quite young

There are strange things happ'ning in Dartymoor Forest—
Christopher Bobbin went there with Doris.
The cairn on High Willhays grows taller each year.
"The whole of the Forest will sink, I fear",
                    Says Doris.

There are strange things happ'ning in Dartymoor Forest—
Christopher Bobbin went there with Doris.
They've hidden the trig point on Rippon Tor.
"I wonder whatever they did it for",
                    Says Doris.

There are strange things happ'ning in Dartymoor Forest—
Christopher Bobbin went there with Doris.
We found a letterbox right on the ground.
"I expect the postman is coming around",
                    Says Doris.

There are strange things happ'ning in Dartymoor Forest—
Christopher Bobbin went there with Doris.
On a tor by a mire lives a wily old fox.
"One of the Rangers looks after his box",
                    Says Doris.

There are strange things happ'ning in Dartymoor Forest—
Christopher Bobbin went there with Doris.
In a shed near Row Tor was a little old train.
"I don't think it'll ever get moving again",
                    Says Doris.

There are strange things happ'ning in Dartymoor Forest—
Christopher Bobbin went there with Doris.
We clambered up to the Queen of the Tors,
But no-one came out. "She must be indoors",
                    Says Doris.

The Snipe

LETTERBOXOLOGY
and
ORNITHOLOGY

make good companions on a moorland walk.

As well as these two stamps others
depicting Owls, Buzzards, Crows,
Ravens, Kestrels, Sparrowhawks,
Grouse, Dippers, and Larks may
all be found, together of course
with their avian counterparts.

The scene here is along the O
Brook in whose valley Heron and
Snipe may often be seen, though
it is admitted that only one of
these letterboxes is anywhere near
the bridge illustrated.

Round-leaved Crowfoot

GREY HERON

FIND ME A TOR

The Dartmoor equivalent of "Home on the Range"

Oh find me a tor that the maps all ignore,

Where the skylarks and ravens still play,

Where no sound is heard save the call of a bird,

For the highway is five miles away.

Rest here all alone,

Where the pipits and wheatears still stay,

Where no sound is heard but the song of a bird,

For the grockles are five miles away.

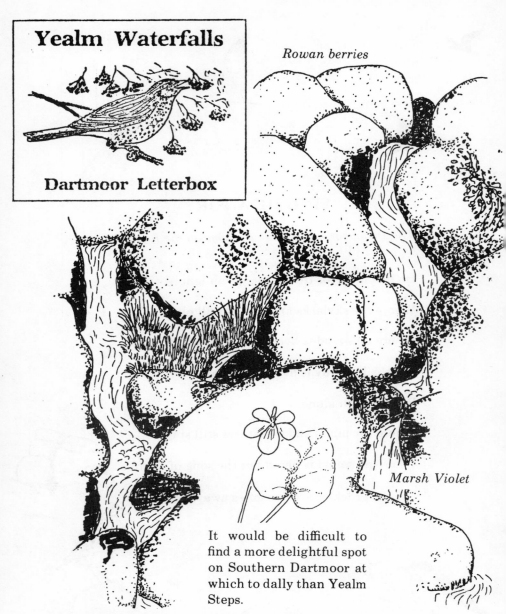

Yealm Waterfalls

Dartmoor Letterbox

Rowan berries

Marsh Violet

It would be difficult to find a more delightful spot on Southern Dartmoor at which to dally than Yealm Steps.

Here on a bright day are birds, butterflies, flowers, berries, and little tinkling cascades. Downstream the views are wide, and upstream an hour's stroll will take you to Yealm Head and back again.

There is a blowing house below the falls and another one above. Each contains two mould-stones which are well worth inspecting.

AVON DAM

For those seeking a pleasant and easy walk on Dartmoor it would
be hard to recommend a better one than the mile and a half stroll
from Shipley Bridge to Avon Dam. A 100 foot high barrage such as
this is inevitably ugly, but the pattern of water tumbling down the
spillway makes a fascinating moving picture to hold one's attention
for a long time. The reservoir filled about 30 years ago and has an
area of about 300 acres.

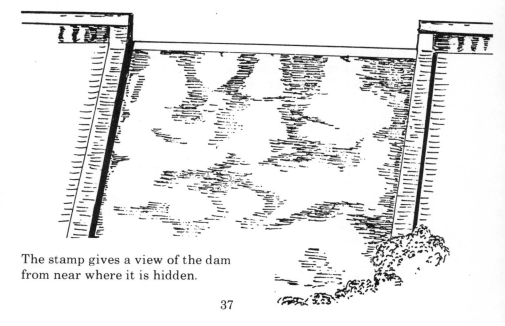

The stamp gives a view of the dam
from near where it is hidden.

KITTY JAY

To be sung, sadly, to the tune of "Billy Boy"

"Where have you been all the night, Kitty Jay, Kitty Jay?"
"Where have you been all the night, O Kitty Jay?"
"I've been tucked up nice and warm
With young Harry at the farm,
    And young Harry promised to marry
    Me, his charming Kitty Jay".

"Oh, don't put your trust in men, Kitty Jay, Kitty Jay,
Oh, don't put your trust in men, dear Kitty Jay.
For he's changed his mind since then
And you'll not see him again,
    So young Harry never will marry
    You, my charming Kitty Jay".

What a dastard to betray Kitty Jay, Kitty Jay,
What a dastard to betray poor Kitty Jay.
Now this fills her with dismay
'Cos she's in the family way,
    And young Harry never will marry
    Her, O wretched Kitty Jay.

"You've been taken for a ride, Kitty Jay, Kitty Jay,
You've been taken for a ride, poor Kitty Jay".
"Since I'm not to be a bride
I'll resort to suicide,
    'Cos young Harry never will marry
    Me, his lovesick Kitty Jay".

She was buried on the hill, Kitty Jay, Kitty Jay,
She is buried on the hill, is Kitty Jay.
She lies sleeping on the hill
'Mong the flowers that blossom still,
    So take pity now upon Kitty,
    Young and foolish Kitty Jay.

Towards the end of the 18th Century a girl called Kitty Jay lived not far from here. She was the sweetheart of a young man who worked at Canna Farm, and unwisely she allowed him to seduce her. Finding herself pregnant—and possibly abandoned—she hanged herself in the barn there.

It was forbidden to bury suicides in hallowed ground so her grave was dug here at a crossroads to prevent the Devil from claiming her . . . and here she still lies, where a track crosses the road half a mile or so Northwest of Hound Tor.

You will always find fresh flowers on her grave, but to find this letterbox you must search high on the hill to the Southwest.

APPLES AND WORTLES   Another version of the Kitty Jay story.

This one has an Irish flavour and is to be sung to the tune "Cockles and Mussels"

In Manaton village
Where the girls all eat porrage
I first set my eyes on sweet Kitty O'Shea,
As she pushed an old barrow
Along the lanes narrow,
    Crying "Apples and wortles! Just ripe to eat O!
    Just ripe to eat O! Just ripe to eat O!"
    Crying "Apples and wortles just ripe to eat O".

I soon found young Kitty
So tender and pretty
We tasted Eve's apple, then got led astray.
But she pushed that old barrow
Along the lanes narrow,
    Crying "Apples and wortles! Just ripe to eat O!
    Just ripe to eat O! Just ripe to eat O!"
    Crying "Apples and wortles just ripe to eat O".

But oh I'd much rather
Not yet be a father,
So "Goodbye" I said to poor Kitty O'Shea,
While she pushed her old barrow
Along the lanes narrow,
    Crying "Apples and wortles! Just ripe to eat O!
    Just ripe to eat O! Just ripe to eat O!"
    Crying "Apples and wortles just ripe to eat O".

Since this brought her hope's end
She hanged on a rope's end,
And that caused the death of poor Kitty O'Shea.
Who once pushed a barrow
Along the lanes narrow,
    Crying "Apples and wortles! Just ripe to eat O!
    Just ripe to eat O! Just ripe to eat O!"
    Crying "Apples and wortles just ripe to eat O".

We never were wedded,
And now she's embedded
In earth all alone by the public highway.
But her ghost wheels her barrow
Along the lanes narrow,
    Crying "Apples and wortles! Just ripe to eat O!
    Just ripe to eat O! Just ripe to eat O!"
    Crying "Apples and wortles just ripe to eat O".

40

LETTERBOXING

naturally appeals to outdoor groups. Scouts, Guides, Cubs and Brownies have all placed boxes on the Moor.

This house was once a peat cutter's dwelling, and a more lonely, desolate spot can hardly be imagined. The house is named on the map, which also shows that a peat pass comes up the hill towards it from the Southwest. This is blanket bog country and the broad gently sloping hill offers soggy but not dangerous walking.

For those who enjoy wide vistas the view from here is stupendous. Not only are the rolling fens and greatest heights of Dartmoor visible, but in clear weather the lines of Exmoor and the Haldons can also be made out.

Stat's House

One end of the building is square and the other round. Inside a fireplace and a smaller recess are still intact. Pause while you are here and contemplate the 'amenities' which the occupant had at hand . . . water, sanitation, light, heat . . . letterbox. The last is not of course in or too near, the house.

41

The Red Grouse

Ling

The Red Grouse was long thought to be the only species of bird wholly restricted to the British Isles, but ornithologists now consider it to be only a race of the more widespread European Willow Grouse. They are not common on Dartmoor, but may sometimes be put up high on the open moor.

The males often select both mate and territory in the Autumn, and for most of the Winter the pair will remain on the territory. The nest is on the ground and a disturbed female will seak to lead possible enemies away from her young. Their food is chiefly Ling but Rushes, berries, and insects may also be taken.

This letterbox is of course in Grouse territory, above the valley of the West Okement.

For many generations peat was the staple fuel for all who lived or worked on the Moor. Its deepest formation is in the two blanket bogs of the North and South Moors and from these areas peat cutters used regular tracks to transport the dried peat to home or blowing house. This track from South Zeal to Hangingstone Hill can still be followed for most of its way.

The letterbox commemorating the peatcutters is somewhere on the flank of Cosdon, in sight of the track.

Another interesting view from this spot is of the village of South Zeal. The hedge lines show very clearly the field system of the 14th century. The narrow 'burgage' plots, originally one to each family, are still largely intact.

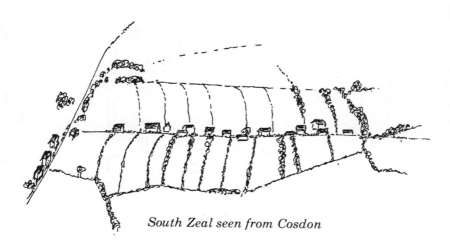

South Zeal seen from Cosdon

For most of the 19th century this farm was actively engaged in rabbit warrening. The buries for the rabbits can still be seen, but the letterbox is not so easily found.

These meagre ruins and a sturdy Sycamore are about all that is now left of the farm . . .

HUNTINGDON WARREN FARM

. . . though the house was still standing in the 1950's

Daffodils planted near the farmhouse years ago still bloom in the Spring.

DAFFOBOXES

*There are plenty of Daffodils on Dartmoor,
but what would Wordsworth have thought
about all these boxes?*

I fluttered aimless as a kite
That's come to grief among the rocks
When lo! I spotted something white
That looked just like an icecream box,
Beneath a boulder, pushed well back
And stuffed inside a plastic sack.

So crouching on the muddy ground
I pulled it out to have a look;
Released the lid, and inside found
A stamp, a pad, a soggy book.
As these I saw with just a glance
My heart with joy began to dance.

Now oft when o'er the Moor I pass
In vacant or in pensive mood
These boxes tumble on the grass
To break a spell of solitude.
And then my heart with passion rocks
And dances with a letterbox.

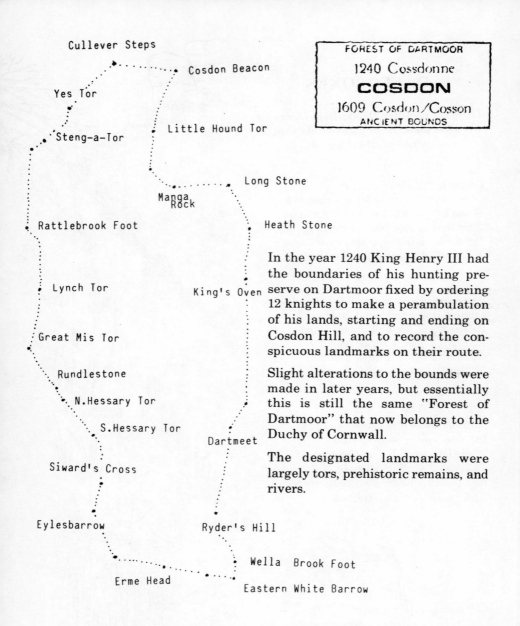

Cullever Steps

Cosdon Beacon

Yes Tor

Little Hound Tor

Steng-a-Tor

Long Stone

Manga Rock

Rattlebrook Foot

Heath Stone

Lynch Tor

King's Oven

Great Mis Tor

Rundlestone

N.Hessary Tor

S.Hessary Tor

Dartmeet

Siward's Cross

Eylesbarrow

Ryder's Hill

Wella Brook Foot

Erme Head

Eastern White Barrow

FOREST OF DARTMOOR
1240 Cossdonne
COSDON
1609 Cosdon/Cosson
ANCIENT BOUNDS

In the year 1240 King Henry III had the boundaries of his hunting preserve on Dartmoor fixed by ordering 12 knights to make a perambulation of his lands, starting and ending on Cosdon Hill, and to record the conspicuous landmarks on their route.

Slight alterations to the bounds were made in later years, but essentially this is still the same "Forest of Dartmoor" that now belongs to the Duchy of Cornwall.

The designated landmarks were largely tors, prehistoric remains, and rivers.

A series of letterboxes is to be found along the Forest boundary shown on this map.

THE
PERAMBULATION

A small blowing house might have looked like this

Mould stone   *Mortar stone*

Round about the 14th century the blowing house came into general use for tin processing, and along many valleys the ruins of these buildings can be found. The banks of the Walkham North of Merrivale are an excellent area to explore for such ruins. Within about a mile there are three to be found.

The source of power was invariably water from a leat. This turned a wheel which operated two other mechanisms: heavy stamps to crush the ore (already broken into small lumps), and bellows which kept the fire at the required heat. These three blowing houses will provide good examples of the structure, wheelpit, mortar stones in which the ore was crushed, a float stone into which the molton tin was run, and mould stones in which the ingots were formed. An ingot, if it filled the mould, would weigh about 200lbs. At two of the sites much smaller sample moulds can also be seen.

This letterbox is not far from one of these blowing houses.

Yes Tor

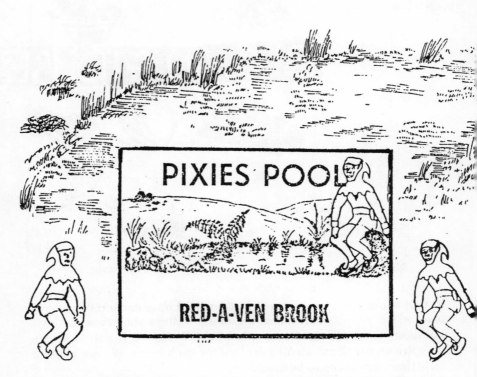

PIXIES POOL

RED-A-VEN BROOK

This delightful pool lies near the source of Red-a-ven Brook under High Willhays. It always holds water and on one side is a bank just right for resting on to pass a sunshiny hour.

Pixies, or Piskies, are inseparable from Dartmoor legend. Even William Crossing, better known for his "Guide", produced in 1890 a booklet subtitled "Glimpses of Elfin Haunts and Antics", nearly 60 pages of entrancing reading.

Here is an imaginative letterbox which supplies three stamps— frame and title, pool scene, and pixie—which may be combined in any way the finder likes.

BATTLE HYMN OF THE PIXIES

To be sung gloriously to one of the rousing tunes of
"Mine eyes have seen the glory",
but NOT "John Brown's Body"

Mine eyes have seen the glory of the pixies by the road,
They are standing there on Dartmeet Hill with toadstool, frog and
   toad,
They are better far then Tupperware and just as good as Spode,
  So tourists, come and buy.
    Glory, glory, grockle-ooya,
    Glory, glory, grockle-ooya,
    Glory, glory, grockle-ooya,
     O, tourists come and buy.

You can see them waiting patiently near New Bridge on
  the Dart,
They are playing in a gateway fit to captivate your heart,
You could liven up your garden with form of modern art,
  So tourists, come and buy.
    Glory, glory, grockle-ooya,
    Glory, glory, grockle-ooya,
    Glory, glory, grockle-ooya,
     O, tourists come and buy.

Down at Wid'combe in the valley they are almost hominoid,
At the cafe and the carpark there are lots of them employed,
They will gaze into your camera with expressions anthropoid,
  So tourists, come and buy.
    Glory, glory, grockle-ooya,
    Glory, glory, grockle-ooya,
    Glory, glory, grockle-ooya,
     O, tourists come and buy.

When you go to see the Prison they'll be sitting in a shop,
Midst the teacloths and the ices all entreating you to stop,
You can buy a plastic pixie while you suck a lollipop,
  So tourists, come and buy.
    Glory, glory, grockle-ooya,
    Glory, glory, grockle-ooya,
    Glory, glory, grockle-ooya,
     O, tourists come and buy.

49

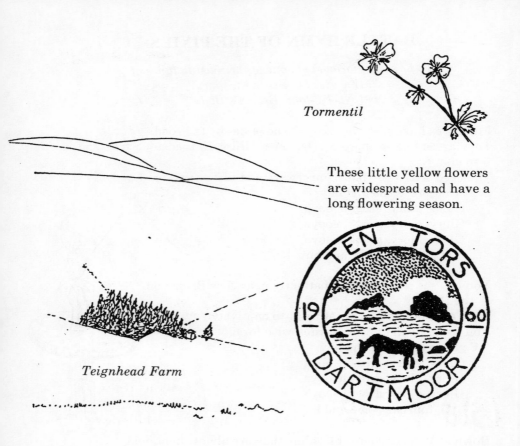

Tormentil

These little yellow flowers are widespread and have a long flowering season.

Teignhead Farm

SITTAFORD TOR may not be one of the most magnificent climbs on Dartmoor, but for those who are interested in the annual "Ten Tors" event it is well worth a visit.

The view to the North includes, not far away, the cluster of conifers round Teignhead Farm. It was here, in September 1959 that several army officers were camped while supervising a military exercise. The nature of the exercise led one of them, Captain Joyner, to conceive the idea of a similar event for younger people. Thus was born the "Ten Tor" concept, and the first trek took place a year later. The assembly point was then at Denbury and the distance to be covered was 55 miles.

The scope of the "Ten Tors" has since widened and other changes have been made, but SITTAFORD TOR has been used as a checkpoint more often than any other tor.

Bench Tor

Dartmoor Matchsticks

Dr. Blackalls Drive

While you are searching for the letter-box stoop to admire the tiny red-tipped lichens known as Dartmoor Matchsticks which grow on this hillside.

This drive runs along the hillside high above the River Dart opposite Bench Tor. The gradient is easy and the view magnificent. The track was made by Doctor Blackall, once Lord of the Manor of Spitchwick, as a scenic drive. One end is at Mel Tor corner and the other on the road Southeast of Poundsgate.

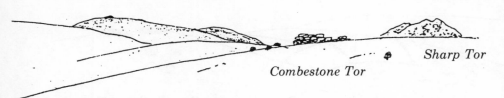

Sharp Tor

Combestone Tor

The skyline seen from Sally's letterbox

Tom and Sally's House

Jolly Lane Cot today

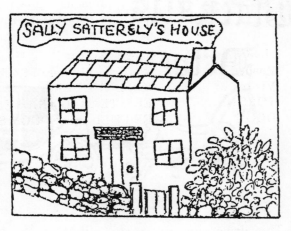

This house, dating from 1832, was the last to be built on the Moor in one day. Custom decreed that if this could be done and a fire lit in the hearth by dusk then the home would belong to its owner for ever.

The house still stands, now with two storeys, by the road below the Forest Inn and is called "Jolly Lane Cot".

To find the letterbox you will have to walk up the valley of the O Brook until you come to the view above.

BOXOES

There are no quinquiremes, stately Spanish galleons,
or dirty British coasters on Dartmoor . . .

. . . but there are other kinds of vessels.

Iron ammunition box from H.M. Army
Dug into a peat hag on Black Ridge bog,
Visited by BOG TROTTERS,
MUDLARKS, SODDEN BOGGERS,
LONE WOLF, EYE SPY, ONE MAN AND
    HIS DOG.

Flexi-plastic white box made to hold icecream
Hidden 'neath a boulder by a lonely tree,
Visited by SCORPIO,
PENTWINS, BOXTANIST,
APPEAL O' BELLS, JEMIMA, and EWE
    AND ME.

Heavy moulded cylinder from Brit Drug Houses
Pushed into a narrow crack in Bonehill Rocks,
Visited by DARTMOOR BOUNDERS,
TORQUAY TREKKERS, TEABAG TRAILERS,
DOG TIRED, BOOTEE FULL, and SOGGY SOX.

Legis Tor Vermin Trap

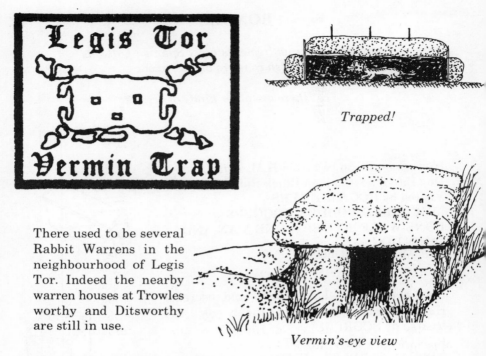

Trapped!

Vermin's-eye view

There used to be several Rabbit Warrens in the neighbourhood of Legis Tor. Indeed the nearby warren houses at Trowlesworthy and Ditsworthy are still in use.

This trap is close to the summit rocks on the Southern side. The lower drawing shows how a stoat or weasel would be encouraged to take the easy way through the tunnel rather than clamber over the boulders. The three holes in the cover-stone were for a contrivance to operate the slate shutters at each end. The exact method of operation is not known, but presumably an animal passing through would operate some kind of trip mechanism.

The letterbox? Well, it's not inside the trap.

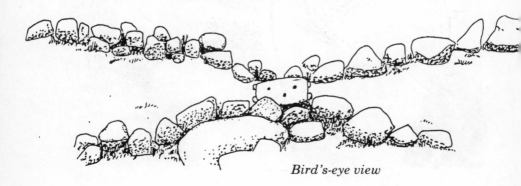

Bird's-eye view

Higher Halstock Farm

1890 - 1976

AGATHA CHRISTIE

"The Mousetrap" and "The Water Babies" would seem to have little to do with Dartmoor, but in fact both authors were familiar with the moorland scene. Agatha Christie was a frequent visitor here—the book in the letterbox (from where the farm above can be . seen) contains a photograph of her having a picnic on the Moor. Charles Kingsley was born at Holne Vicarage, and the letterbox is, appropriately, near Holne Moor Leat.

THE WATER BABIES

Holne Moor Leat

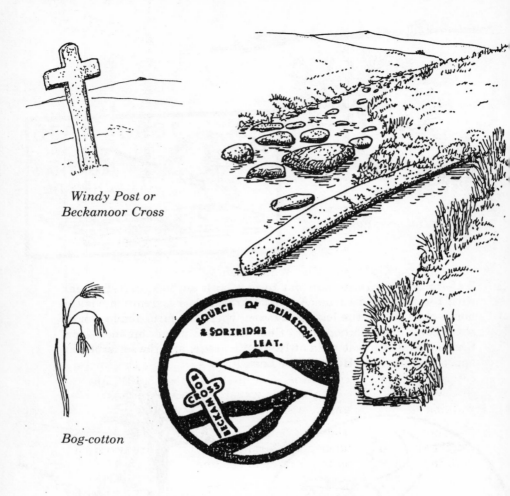

Windy Post or
Beckamoor Cross

Bog-cotton

Leat walking has much appeal: it provides fresh air and exercise with hardly ever any arduous hill-climbing.

The Grimstone and Sortridge Leat comes off the right bank of the Walkham west of Great Mis Tor, and runs for about 6 miles to supply water to the manors after which it is named. It flows round the flank of Great Staple Tor and then through Merrivale Quarry, where for a short way it cannot be followed. The leat then crosses under the road, over Beckamoor Brook, and on between Barn Hill and Beckamoor Cross, more usually called Windypost.

The stamp incorporates several of these items. The letterbox is in the vicinity of the leat's source.

OLD RAILWAY

Not far from Princetown the great quarries at Foggin Tor, Swell Tor, King's Tor, and Ingra Tor once supplied fine granite for many well-known buildings—London Bridge and Nelson's Column among them. The need to transport the stone to Plymouth for onward passage by sea resulted, in 1823, in the first iron railway in Devon Sixty years later the Great Western Railway rebuilt the line and introduced steam locomotives. The last train ran in 1956 and the line was closed. The high moorland part of the route makes easy walking through magnificent scenery.

It is not surprising that the imagination of letterboxes has been caught up in the romance of the "iron horses". Here are two stamps both to be found along this stretch of the line.

This bridge over the railway allows stock access from one side of the line to the other.

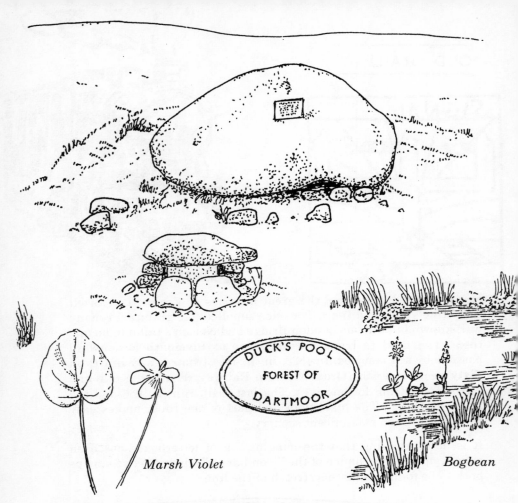

Marsh Violet

DUCK'S POOL
FOREST OF
DARTMOOR

Bogbean

There are only two fixed letterboxes on Dartmoor, this and the one at Cranmere. They are both marked on the map.

Here a number of small pools lie in a boggy hollow like a huge soupbowl about 100 yards across. Some of the pools are Sphagnum filled and only prove to be watery if you try to cross them. Others have a few square yards of open water. In late Spring and Summer spikes of Bogbean rise above the surface and Marsh Violets spangle the Bog-mosses with tiny splashes of colour.

The letterbox was placed here in 1938 to commemorate the life and work of William Crossing who had died ten years earlier.

Another letterbox, commemorating this indispensable author in a different way, is also included in this book.

BOX FEVER

Some people must go down to the seas again, but . . .

I must go out on the moors again, to the rolling hills and the rocks,
And all I ask is a good clue to another letterbox;
And a long tramp o'er distant hills, and a soft breeze blowing,
And a kind sun, or a rain-proof mac, and the waymarks showing.

I must go out on the moors again, to search for a letterbox
In a peat face, or a dark crack among the lichened rocks;
And all I ask is a helpful hint to save the time a-seeking,
And quick success, and a stout box with a lid not leaking.

I must go out on the moors again, where the raven lives, and the fox,
And the grouse dwell, and the larks nest, to find a letterbox;
And all I ask is a dry book where happy thoughts are penned
By Diptford Hound to start with, and Kilroy at the end.

59

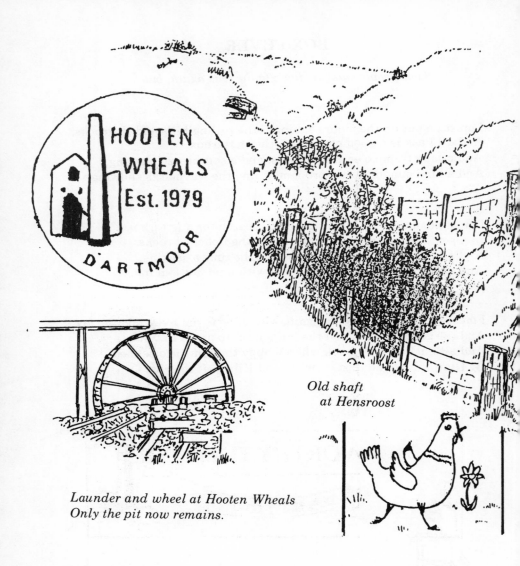

HOOTEN WHEALS Est. 1979 DARTMOOR

Old shaft at Hensroost

Launder and wheel at Hooten Wheals Only the pit now remains.

Old mines have a fascination for some people. An area in which intriguing relics are still to be found is at Hooten Wheals and Hensroost in the O valley. Shafts, wheelpits, buddles, gullies, aqueducts, and tracks extend over a large area. In the early years of this century the sites were amalgamated and became known as Hexworthy Mine.

Two letterboxes are to be found in the area, but a warning to walk carefully among the diggings should be well heeded.

The wheelpit at the Drylake site

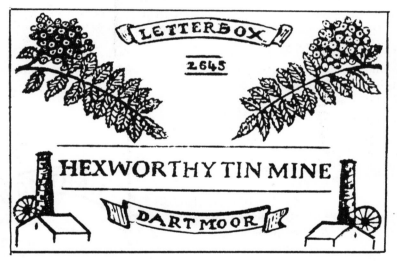

The delightful 3-mile long valley of the O Brook is a favourite with walkers, picnickers, and letterboxers. For many centuries tin streaming or mining has been carried on along the whole length of the river. At its foot there are two blowing houses; in the middle reaches great gullies, wheelpits, and dressing floors; and in the upper region are several deep shafts. It was not until the early 1920's that work finally ceased.

The Forest Boundary runs along the lower half of the O Brook.

Devil's Tor and Beardown Man

Devil's Tor, Devil's Pan, Devil's Bridge, Devil's Gully, Devil's Kitchen, Devil's Elbow . . . Old Nick certainly gets around the Moor quite a bit . . . and letterboxes seem keen to follow him!

The mighty menhir that stands near the tor is known as Beardown Man. The most impressive view of it is edge on, when it appears unbelievably thin.

 The purplish-blue DEVIL'S-BIT SCABIOUS is to be found on Dartmoor in late Summer and early Autumn.

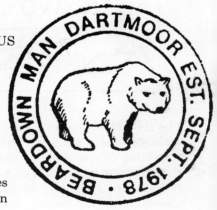

This is a lonely spot. North of here lies some of the most difficult walking on the Moor. Bogs and mists are to be feared, but bears and devils should cause little concern.

Watern Tor seen from Shovel Down

The Thurlestone through the tor

WATERN TOR and the THURLESTONE have been recorded landmarks ever since the Forest of Dartmoor was described in 1240.

Along its western foot the Walla Brook runs in a narrow valley. Here in this remote spot tin streamers, fairies, and letterboxers have all gathered for different purposes.

Combe Fairies

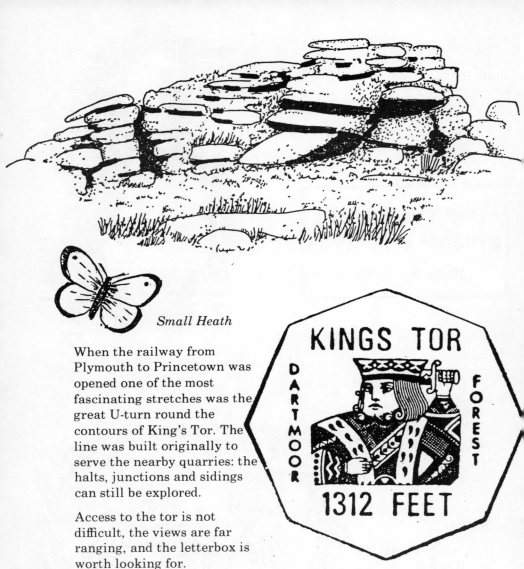

Small Heath

When the railway from Plymouth to Princetown was opened one of the most fascinating stretches was the great U-turn round the contours of King's Tor. The line was built originally to serve the nearby quarries: the halts, junctions and sidings can still be explored.

Access to the tor is not difficult, the views are far ranging, and the letterbox is worth looking for.

KINGS TOR

DARTMOOR FOREST

1312 FEET

Old railway west of the tor

BOX HARVEST

A harvest time song that may be sung to the tune
"We plough the fields and scatter . . ."

We scour the Moor for boxes
Well scattered o'er the land,
Just put there for our pleasure
By someone else's hand.
We brave the snow in Winter
To cross the rough terrain,
We climb the tors in Summer
Through driving sleet and rain.

CHORUS: All these little boxes
In secret places dwell,
So keep them dry, O keep them dry,
And hide them well.

We search for letterboxes
In places far and near,
We cross a hundred rivers
By boulder, ford, or weir.
The bogs and mists surround us,
Grey clouds pass overhead,
But in the sky a lark sings
To cheer the path we tread.

CHORUS

We thank the many people
Who hide these boxes small.
We spend our lives out hunting,
Yet cannot find them all,
For some are hid in clitter
And some in peaty banks,
But whereso'er we find them
Accept our grateful thanks

CHORUS

65

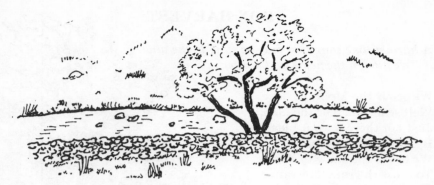

Wall by the River Taw near Steeperton

'Grounders' at a wall base

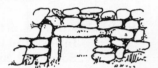

Sheep creep in a wall

The dry-stone walls of the granite lands are always worth examining. The construction of those in good repair must often be a source of admiration for their builders. The huge size of some of the 'grounders' makes one wonder how they were lifted and shifted.

One well-known wall on the Northern Moor runs right over the Belstone Tors. It is called Irishman's Wall because it was built, in the last century, by an Irish gang said to have worked bare-footed. However when the wall was nearing completion the indignant villagers assembled one night and toppled enough of it over to dissuade the builders from further attempts at establishing a 'Little Ireland' on Dartmoor.

The Long Wall North Dartmoor

The stamp in this letterbox is in 3 parts, so that keen collectors who carry more than one pad may arrange the parts in different colours according to their fancy.

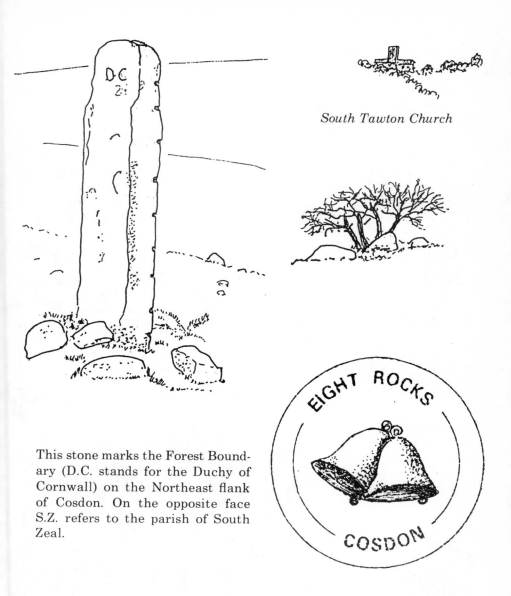

South Tawton Church

This stone marks the Forest Boundary (D.C. stands for the Duchy of Cornwall) on the Northeast flank of Cosdon. On the opposite face S.Z. refers to the parish of South Zeal.

Near here years ago stood a fine stone circle known as the Eight Rocks, and the story goes that they would dance whenever they heard the bells of South Tawton—the church to be seen in the distance to the North.

The stones, alas, were all removed, probably early in the last century, to be used in building walls for a new enclosure.

Bear necessities

HONEYBAG is a name that catches the imagination. There are two letterboxes on this tor. Each interprets the name differently and delightfully.

WISTMANS WOOD

the druids woz 'ere

WISTMAN'S WOOD has been known as one of the Moor's curiosities for a long time.

This almost impenetrable oakwood, whose floor is a mass of enormous boulders; whose trees grow at all angles from horizontal to vertical; whose every surface—rock or bark—is densely covered with mosses, liverworts, lichens, ferns, rushes, flowers, and even treelets; whose canopy of twigs and leaves is only a few feet above head height, has excited people's imagination and fears throughout the ages.

Some say the name is derived from "Wiseman", others from "Welshman", and others from "using maen coed" (which means 'the stony wood by the water').

The botanical interest of the wood is very great. Visit it if you have not yet done so, and find the nearby letterbox if you can.

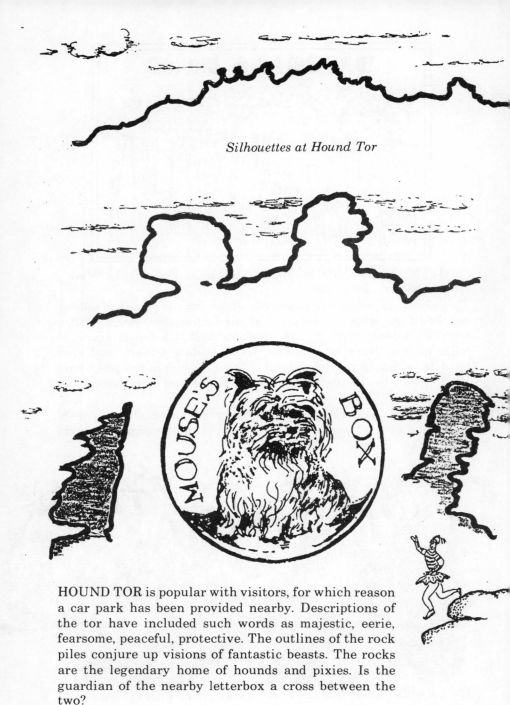

Silhouettes at Hound Tor

HOUND TOR is popular with visitors, for which reason a car park has been provided nearby. Descriptions of the tor have included such words as majestic, eerie, fearsome, peaceful, protective. The outlines of the rock piles conjure up visions of fantastic beasts. The rocks are the legendary home of hounds and pixies. Is the guardian of the nearby letterbox a cross between the two?

MACGODFREY'S BOX

Old MacDonald had a farm but . . .

Old Macgodfrey had a box,
E I E I O.
And in that box there was a "Mouse",
E I E I O.
With a wuff wuff here and a wuff wuff there,
Here a wuff, there a wuff, everywhere a wuff wuff,
E I E I O.

Old Macgodfrey had a box,
E I E I O.
And in that box there was a bee,
E I E I O.
With a buzz buzz here and a buzz buzz there,
Here a buzz, there a buzz, everywhere a buzz buzz,
E I E I O.

Old Macgodfrey had a box,
E I E I O.
And in that box there was a fly,
E I E I O.
With a zzz zzz here and a zzz zzz there,
Here a zzz, there a zzz, everywhere a zzz zzz,
E I E I O.

Old Macgodfrey had a box,
E I E I O.
And in that box there was a slug,
E I E I O.
With a shlsh shlsh here and a shlsh shlsh there,
Here a shlsh, there a shlsh, everywhere a shlsh shlsh,
E I E I O.

Old Macgodfrey had a box,
E I E I O.
And in that box there was a worm,
E I E I O.
With a mmm mmm here and mmm mmm there,
Here a mmm, there a mmm, everywhere a mmm mmm,
E I E I O.

According to legend these stones on Belstone Down are nine local girls who were turned into stone for daring to dance on the Sabbath. It is said that they change places every day at noon: there is certainly photographic evidence that in 1985 one of them had moved into the centre of the circle.

Go and see, and count them!

If you search for the letterbox move well away from the stones.

PUPERS HILL   SOUTH DARTMOOR

LEAD ME FROM DEATH
to LIFE, from FALSEHOOD to TRUTH
✦
LEAD ME FROM DESPAIR
to HOPE, from FEAR to TRUST
✦
LEAD ME FROM HATE
to LOVE, from WAR to PEACE
✦✦✦
LET PEACE FILL OUR HEART
OUR WORLD, OUR UNIVERSE

Prayer for Peace

When a Southwesterly blows across the open moor seek shelter in this little hollow. Here is a tiny haven of calm, a wide view to contemplate, a letterbox to find, and a text to ponder.

The prayer, quoted here in full, was first promulgated in 1981 and has achieved wide use among many nations.

Whortleberries

Cross-leaved Heath

73

SMUGGLERS HOLE 19·87

Northeast of Stalldown Barrow a tiny stream runs down to the Erme, and near its foot the O.S. mark "Downing's House". This is one of the few beehive huts on the Moor which still have a roof. Originally built by the tinners for storing tools and perhaps ingots, it is said to have been later used as a cache for smuggled brandy. Hence its present name.

TINKERS BRIDGE

Tinker's Bridge, once nearby, has been replaced by a modern one to carry the track that runs up the Erme valley.

These two interesting spots, close to each other, are easily missed— so are the letterboxes not far away.

Cairn on High Willes
in 1987

In 1971 it looked like this

Here we are on the highest ridge in the South of England. Not until you reach the Pennines will you find a higher mountain. The spelling of the name has several variations, and so has the recorded height, but it is certain that these are the only two tors on Dartmoor to top 2,000 feet. High Willes (the spelling preferred here) is usually put at 2,038 feet, while Yes Tor is about 8 feet lower. In metres the heights are 621 and 619. However as can be seen from the two sketches, dated 1971 and 1987, the cairn on top is growing!

The old stamp

Yes Tor
seen from High Willes

At one time the letterbox was cemented into the West face near the cairn. It has now been moved to a more discreet distance, and a new stamp provided.

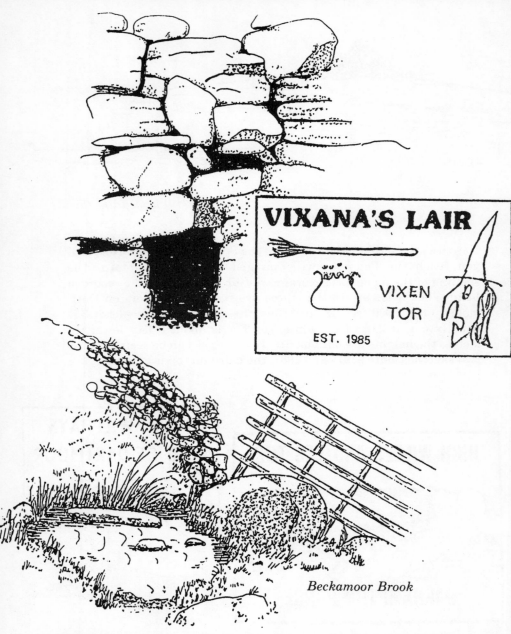

VIXANA'S LAIR

VIXEN TOR

EST. 1985

Beckamoor Brook

VIXANA was a witch who lived in this cave on Vixen Tor. She used to lure travellers to their death in the bog in the valley below.

The letterbox too is down in the valley, for fear that searchers should misguidedly pry into her lair.

THE SONG OF LOWAWATHA

by H. W. Shortfellow

Should you ask me, "Whence these
   stories?"
I should answer, I should tell you,
"From the misty moors of Devon,
From the torrents, woods, and hillsides
Where the Dipper and the Wheatear
Make their home among the boulders."

There was born my Lowawatha;
Spent his childhood, grew to manhood,
Learned to love the tors and rivers.

Once a piskie by the Walkham
Fell into the rushing water.
Lowawatha entered boldly,
Plucked him from the swirling current,
Rescued him from being carried
To the shores of Gitche Gumee,
To the white-waved Big Sea Water.
For this deed of noble valour,
"I will give you", said the piskie,
"Power to see through mist and darkness.
Use it well to travel safely,
Helping others out of danger."

Lowawatha thanked the piskie,
Journeyed on across the moorland
Till he came to Merrivallee
Where he tarried in the hostel.
There he heard the story spoken,
Heard the tale of foul Vixana,
Hideous witch of Vixentoree
She who watched from Vixen's summit
Waiting for a lonely trav'ler
Coming down from Windiposta
To the mire of Beckamooree.
Conjured mists across the pathway,
Cackled as the hapless trav'ler
Stumbled into quaking bogland,
Sank beneath the em'rald Sphagnum.

Thither then strode Lowawatha,
Took the path to Samfordspinee,
Took the path he knew would lead him
Through the mire of Beckamooree,
Past the beetling, craggy rock-pile,
Past the home of vile Vixana.

When Vixana saw him striding
Through the Asphodel and Bogmoss
She with magic brought a mist down,
Hid the mire and path across it.

Lowawatha, nothing hindered,
Quickly gained the rocky hillside,
Reached the summit from the hindside,
Saw Vixana peering downward
Waiting for his cries of anguish
From the wat'ry bog beneath them.

"Hi!" said Lowawatha softly,
Waited till she turned towards him,
Hurled her off with mighty effort,
Heard her shriek as down she hurtled,
Plunged beneath the floating Sphagnum,
There to bide for ever after.

Vixen Tor

77

Conies Down Tor

Lydford Tor

At the foot of Conies Down the River Cowsic is joined by Conies Down Water in a hollow known as Broad Hole. Just above the confluence Travellers' Ford, set in delightful surroundings, makes an easy river crossing.

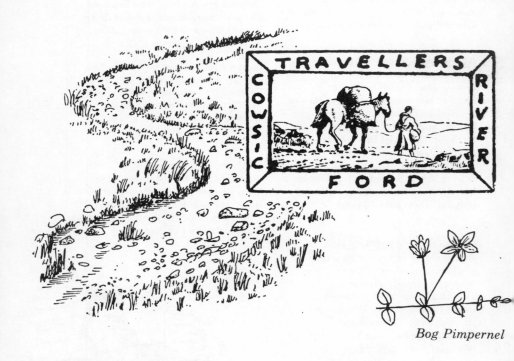

Bog Pimpernel

The track is the Lych Way, or the Way of the Dead. Coming from Lydford it skirts Conies Down, crosses the Cowsic, and along a well-worn stretch mounts the hill towards Lydford Tor. After the year 1260 this track was no longer used to carry the dead to Lydford from hamlets to the Southeast, but a great deal of traffic still came this way, for at Lydford were castle, prison, and the Forest courts.

Hangingstone Hill
on the Southeast horizon

This very shallow hard-bottomed pool, high on the Moor between Cranmere and the Military Road, is, surprisingly, seldom without water. It lies in the blanket bog of Okement Hill, but a hard track leads to it from the East, while from the Western side a peat-pass comes up the hill towards it.

The pool area is also known as Huggaton Court. This name, like Ockerton, is also a variation of Okement.

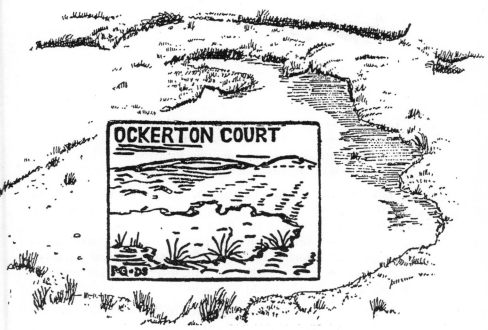

The owner of the nearby letterbox has thoughtfully provided an extra stamp depicting a sunset. So if you are here on a fine evening and carry both a black and a red inkpad you can add a glorious technicolour impression to your collection.

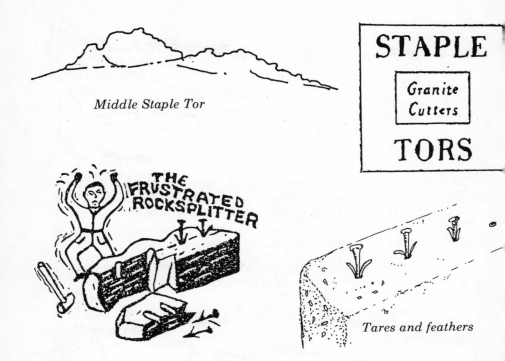

Middle Staple Tor

STAPLE

Granite Cutters

TORS

THE FRUSTRATED ROCKSPLITTER

Tares and feathers

The hill on which the three Staple Tors stand is an excellent one on which to find signs of an important moorland industry of the second half of the 19th century. The nearness of these clitter-strewn slopes to the highway made them an obvious location for the work of splitting and dressing moorstone.

About 1800 the old method of splitting large blocks by driving wedges into grooves was superseded by the "tare and feathers" method. In this operation a row of holes was first drilled along the line of the desired split by using a "jumper" (a large cold chisel). Then a tare was inserted into each hole and wedged with two feathers. The tares were then driven harder into the rock until the stresses set up caused the boulder to split.

Examples of this method of working are to be found all over the Moor, but they are particularly common here.

Two letterboxes remind us of this work, and it is not difficult to find large blocks whose nature frustrated the worker by splitting in the wrong place.

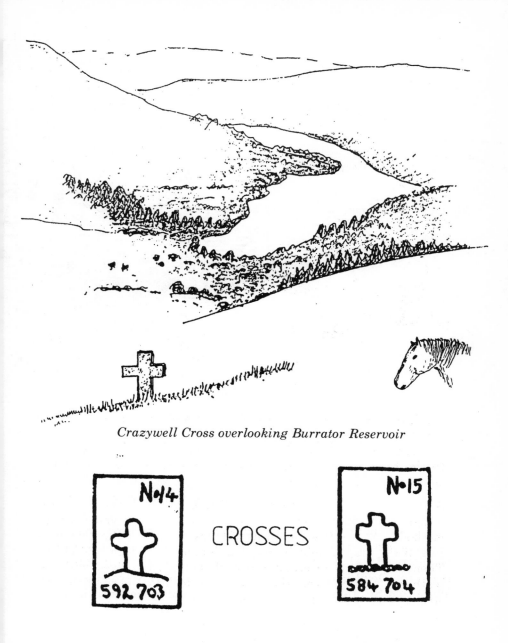

Crazywell Cross overlooking Burrator Reservoir

Nº14

592 703

CROSSES

Nº15

584 704

One of the old monastic routes crossing Dartmoor is marked by a number of crosses. Here on Walkhampton Common are two of them, Newleycombe Cross and Crazywell Cross. Letterboxes associated with them are also to be found on this common.

Brent Tor seen from Paddington's box

Noël

PADDINGTON

There are several legends about the building of St Michael's Church on Brent Tor. One says that a grateful mariner tried to build it on the tor summit but that every night the Devil threw the stones down to the bottom, while another story is that the local people tried to build the church at the foot of the hill but every night the Devil carried the stones to the top. However both tales affirm that St Michael came to the rescue and hurled a rock at the mischief maker causing him to take to his heels.

The tor is not of granite but is of pillow lava formed in a submarine eruption.

Here are two letterbox stamps, one showing the distant view that Paddington has of the tor, while the other is a special Christmas issue.

THE LEGEND OF BRENTOR

The building of the church of St Michael de Rupe

To be sung to the tune "While shepherds watched . . ."

While sailors watched the waves one
night
All standing round the deck
The captain of the ship announced
It soon would be a wreck.

"I fear", said he, "this mighty storm
Will drive us hard aground.
Prepare yourselves to swim, my lads,
We'll not make Plymouth Sound."

But Hugh the merchant raised his voice
And prayed with upstretched hand,
"St Michael, save us, we implore,
And bring us safe to land."

Thus spake good Hugh, and promise
made
That if they came ashore
He'd build a little church for Mike
Upon a Dartmoor tor.

St Michael saw the upraised hands
And heard the merchant's plea.
He took compassion on the ship
And calmed the raging sea.

They steered a course for Plymouth Hoe
And entered Dev'nport dock,
Where Hugh espied some miles inland
A likely looking rock.

Forthwith he hurried, Northward bent,
To keep the vow he'd made.
At Brentor rock he set to work
With hammer, pick, and spade.

For fourteen days his pile of stones
Upon the summit grew.
"Tomorrow morn, if all goes well,
I'll start to build", quoth Hugh.

But Satan came that very night.
Said he, "A trick I'll play."
He lifted up the pile of stones
And flung them far away.

It took poor Hugh the whole next day
To carry back the stones.
When evening came he went to bed
To rest his weary bones.

But once again the Devil came
And played his dirty trick.
Old Hugh took back the stones,
and prayed,
"O help me, please, St Mick."

The third night when the Devil came
He got a big surprise:
St Michael hurled a rock at him
And hit him 'tween the eyes.

No more attempts the Devil made
To hinder valiant Hugh,
Who went ahead with building ops
And saw the project through.

Now if you climb up Brentor hill
To see the glorious view,
Remember there to pause and give
Your thanks to Mike and Hugh.

Church of St Michael de Rupe, Brentor

Vixen Tor across the valley

THE WHEELWRIGHT

Beckamoor Water

This little stream runs below the leat to join the River Walkham beyond Vixen Tor, seen to the Southeast.

This letterbox takes its name from the nearby wheelwright's stone. This lies by the Grimstone Leat on the side of Barn Hill.

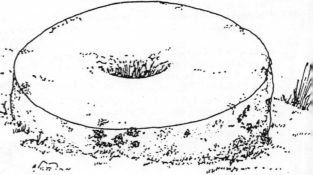

Nearby also are the ruins of a small building known as the Blacksmith's Shop, which probably provided tools and service for the stonecutters working on the slopes of the Staple Tors.

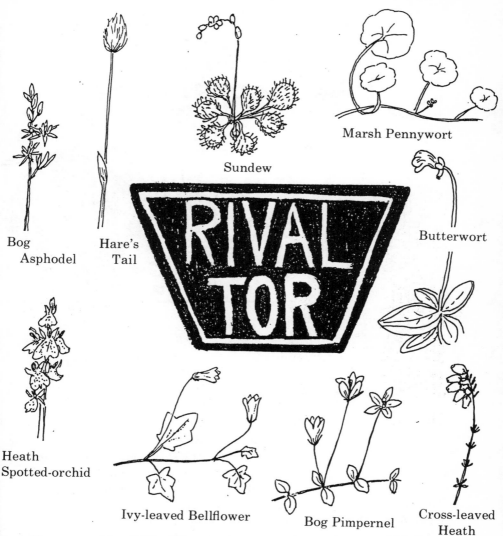

Sundew

Marsh Pennywort

Bog
Asphodel

Hare's
Tail

Butterwort

Heath
Spotted-orchid

Ivy-leaved Bellflower

Bog Pimpernel

Cross-leaved
Heath

No one could call Rival Tor (or Ripper Tor to give it its other name) a great tor, or even a popular one, but being set in the middle of a marshy basin nearly 2 miles across it has an air of isolation that well rewards the effort to attain it.

From the summit a ring of greater tors is seen, and, as much of the intervening ground is also in view, this gives a dreamer on the low granite outcrop a sense of being a long way from the rest of the world. For those who enjoy that experience it is much easier to get here than to the centre of the upland blanket bogs.

There is a letterbox to find, and on the way flowers to enjoy.

B is for
Beautiful
Boundary
Bunny
Bedford

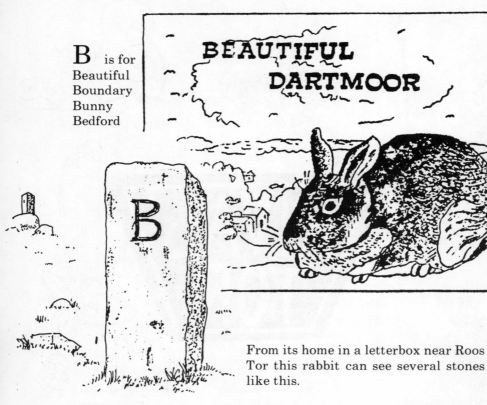

BEAUTIFUL DARTMOOR

Boundary Stone

From its home in a letterbox near Roos Tor this rabbit can see several stones like this.

About 1880 the Duke of Bedford had erected at Roos Tor a number of these inscribed stones, to mark a boundary round the tor within which the sett-makers were not allowed to extract stone for their work—cutting setts for use in paving and cobbling city streets.

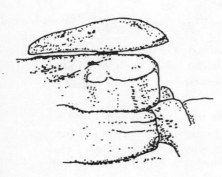

Logan Stone

If your eyes and legs do not lead you to the box then why not exercise your arms by rocking this logan stone on the tor.

STARCH FACTORY
Sheepfold
DARTMOOR

Inside the Sheepfold

This fascinating building, about a mile North of Postbridge, is marked on the map as "The Sheepfold". This name is derived from its use by a Scottish farmer at Teignhead who folded his sheep here in Winter. It seems that he adapted for his own use walls and buildings which were already here. The place had originally been built as a factory by two brothers who planned to produce starch here from locally grown potatoes. This was a project which seems to have failed before it ever got started!

The massive construction of the longer walls is well worth examining. One face of each (the downhill side) has huge uprights spaced at 2–3 yard intervals. Inside are other rows of upright stones arranged differently along opposite walls. At one end is a walled-in entrance, and at the other the remains of a cottage which was burnt down early in the last century.

Part of the outside wall

Meldon Reservoir

BRANSCOMBES
CORN-RIDGE
LOAF

*Branscombe's
Loaf*

On Cornridge stands a mini-tor known as Branscombe's Loaf. This lonely, weather-beaten lump of rock on the open heath makes a goal for a pleasant pilgrimage. The view to the North down the length of Meldon reservoir is a fine one, and to the East, above Black Tor rises the highest ridge in Southern England.

The legend associated with this rock has many minor variations, but all tell how Bishop Branscombe (a real 13th century bishop) was once lost with his chaplain just near here. A stranger approached and offered bread and cheese to the weary travellers. They were about to accept when just in time the chaplain noticed a cloven foot projecting from beneath the stranger's cloak. He cried out and struck the loaf away. The Bishop made the sign of the Cross and the satanic stranger vanished. The loaf still lies here . . . untouched. So does the cheese which you may find nearby.

BISHOP BRANSCOMBE

To be sung to the tune of
"God King Wenceslas"
while walking across Corn Ridge

Bishop Branscombe once set out
From the town of Tavy,
Wined and dined on mead and stout,
Meat, two veg and gravy.
Reg his pageboy went with him,
Helped to keep him merry,
Fortified with Eau de Plym
And a cask of sherry.

Soon they climbed the Western slope,
Toiling through the heather,
But they went on buoyed with hope
Braving wind and weather.
Then their way grew steeper still:
Now they found it tiring:
Plodding on with steadfast will
They were both perspiring.

"Sir, I can't last out the day
Now the wind blows stronger,
I am sure we've lost the way,
I can go no longer."
"Cheer up Reggie", said the Bish,
"I espy a stranger,
Just the person we would wish,
'Tis a Dartmoor Ranger."

On they hurried 'cross the moor,
Stumbling through the clitter,
Oozing sweat from every pore,
Wishing they were fitter.
"Mornin' all", the Ranger said,
"Where be you a-walkin'?"
But the Bish was puffed and red,
Hardly fit for talkin'.

"'Pon my word", the Bishop said,
"Us be tired an' weary,
Trudgin', thirsty and unfed,
O'er this landscape dreary."
"Take this loaf", the stranger cried,
"Put some food within you.
Once you've got it safe inside
You can then continue."

Bish, he took the bread to eat,
Thanked the gen'rous stranger.
Just then Reggie saw the feet
Of the so-called Ranger:
Poking out from 'neath the coat
"Twas not shoes he wore there:
Two feet cloven like a goat
Worthy Reggie saw there.

Sprang he into action quick,
Smashed the loaf asunder,
Hurled invective at Old Nick
In a voice of thunder.
"Well done, Reg", the Bishop cried,
"Thanks for your devotion.
When we reach the other side
You will get promotion."

Satan fled with muttered curse,
"Bother and damnation."
On they plodded, none the worse,
To their destination.
Page and Biship on they went
Through the dreary weather,
Left the loaf without lament
In the purple heather.

Branscombe's
Loaf

Still it lies on Cornridge brow,
Gives this story credit,
'Branscombe's Loaf' they call it now
Though 'tis made of granite.
Page and Bishop they're not here,
They have gone to Heaven,
But Old Nick is much more near,
He still lives in Devon.

NAMESAKES

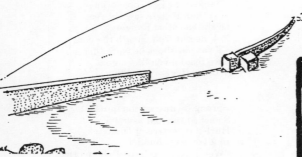

Rock formation on Sharp Tor

Leamansmead beyond the Avon dam

It is natural for people to feel an attraction towards any geographical features that bear their own name.

Such Dartmoor localities as Dick's Well, Simon's Lake, Tom's Lane, Johnson's Cut, Nipper's Hole, and possibly even Jackman's Bottom, are sure to rouse feelings of ownership or at least interest in the heart of their namesakes.

This is an excellent reason to put a letterbox in an appropriate place. Thus the Leaman family have a box somewhere on Leamansmead, and the Sharp family own one on Sharp Tor.

Is there a Mr Willhays or a Mrs Yes among our readers?
Or an enthusiastic youngster named Zeal?

Cranmere is a 'must' at some time for all letterboxers. One of the pleasantest ways of getting there is to walk from Meldon Reservoir up the West Okement.

By the river just Southwest of Vergyland Combe stands a ruined tinners' hut. From here a short stroll across the hillside will bring you to this delightful pool.

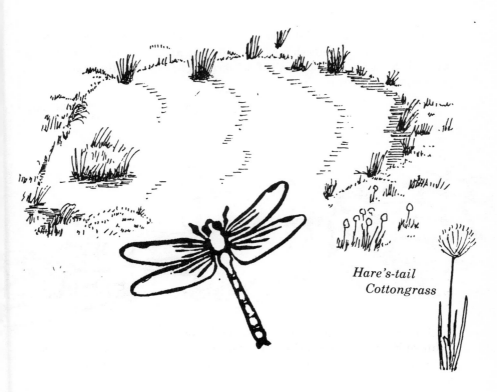

Hare's-tail Cottongrass

Set in the blanket bog, it always contains water. Flowers and sedges surround it, and several species of dragonfly live in its peaty depths or hawk across its surface.

The pool has no name on the map, but the owner of this letterbox has thoughtfully given it one: Dragonfly Pool.

Dartmoor's Industry

MINES AND WORKINGS OF THE PAST

STONE TOR

Most of Dartmoor's industries, however short-lived, have been commemorated by letterboxes, though not all of these are still on site. Here is a recent one of a series chosen to illustrate tin streaming near Stone Tor.

The North wall of Langridge Newtake and Stone Tor

This little tor must surely rank as one of the smallest on the Moor that has a name. Indeed when walking beside the wall into which it is incorporated one could easily miss the tor altogether.

. . . And the letterbox is even easier to miss.

THE SONG OF LETTAWATHA

*Lettawatha was a White Indian
renowned for his exploits on Dartmoor.*

Lo, across the landscape striding,
Map and compass held before him,
Lettawatha climbs the hillsides,
Wades the rivers, scans the torsides,
Stops awhile, consults a booklet,
Sets a dial, turns and gazes;
Then with steadfast paces counted
Strides through heather, gorse, and bracken,
Stumbling not on sheep or boulder
Till the reckoned score is counted.
Now the eager Lettawatha
Casts his questing eye around him,
Seeks a cave beneath a boulder
Closed by rocks whose pristine surface
Neither moss nor lichen cover.
Thus it is the secret's told that
Hidden in that darksome hollow
Lies the goal of his ambition,
Lies the treasure he has yearned for,
Lies a Dartmoor letterbox.

Kes Tor

The Third Boy

The Longstone

The Three Boys

Shovel Down

Milkwort

Shovel Down, S.W. of Kes Tor, is dotted with prehistoric remains. There are half a dozen stone rows, some single, some double, four concentric circles, menhirs, kistvaens, cairns, and possibly the remains of a dolmen. Apart from The Longstone which stands about ten feet high, there are no stones of very impressive size. Some of the rows are well covered in heather and not easy to spot, while others have been robbed for wall building.

Towards the Southern end of the down the O.S. map marks "The Three Boys". Alas, only one now remains, and that is responding slowly to the force of gravity. It has been suggested that they once formed part of a dolmen, as illustrated on the stamp.

Letterboxes of course are never placed in or under any archaeological remains. You will have to hunt around to find this one.

at Merrivale

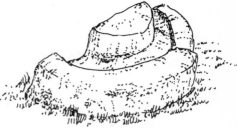

near Sourton Tors

ABANDONED APPLE CRUSHER MERRIVALE

APPLE CRUSHER BOX

Cider making has long been a cottage industry in Devon. Apparatus for crushing the apples has to be heavy and moorstone (surface boulders) is an obvious choice.

Here and there can be found the remains of cider presses which have been shaped and then abandoned. The reasons for this are usually clear—perhaps a split has made the stone useless—but occasionally no obvious fault can be found.

Two of these stones have letterboxes associated with them: the huge edge runner (the upright component) above Merrivale, and the half-trough by the King Way, East of Sourton Tors.

Here are two other similar relics

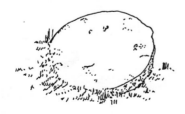

near Rippon Tor

on Haytor Down

IFF

If only Kipling could read this!

If you can plod for miles through mists unbroken
    To rest content upon an unnamed tor,
Or walk for sunlit hours with no word spoken
    Except a skylark singing o'er the moor;

If you can keep your feet and not go sliding
    Off stones that glisten in a laughing stream,
Or through a quaking bog go boldly striding
    To pick your route with confidence supreme;

If you can leap from hag to hag so lightly
    You never soil your jeans with soggy peat;
If you can run and jump and judge it rightly
    And never land with one foot in a leat;

If you have learned the course of Teign and Okement
    By trudging through the mire to where they start;
If you can understand just what the bloke meant
    'Oo zed 'e zee'd zum piskies up the Dart;

    If you abhor to hear the tourists shouting,
        Or watch them flying kites from Haytor Rocks:
    Then get your map and compass for an outing.
    Be off!—On Cut Hill there's a letterbox.

Grid Ref. 5984·8269

Height 603m.

Cut Hill - Dartmoor's Utmost

Peat hags on Cut Hill

For those who want to get away from it all it is usually reckoned that the central summit of the Northern Wilderness is Cut Hill. There is no longer way back to the nearest road from any other moorland height, and even then a beeline to the car is not to be recommended since the hill is surrounded by blanket bog. According to the lastest O.S. map only High Willhays and Yes Tor surpass Cut Hill in height. There is no tor on the summit, just a magnificent view and acres of eroding peat.

Among those who have made the effort to get there two strongly held opinions are held—"I love Cut Hill" and "I hate Cut Hill".

BOUNDSTONES

Across Haytor Down runs a line of boundstones set up by the Duke of Somerset in 1853. They follow the parish boundaries of Bovey, Manaton, and Ilsington. Where these three parishes meet a simpler triangular stone is just marked B, M, and I. The stones are mostly well shaped and each bears an individual name. Running from S.E. to N.W. are Prince Albert, Owlacombe Burrow, William, Old Jack, Victoria, Writenol, Prince of Wales, and Hole Rock.

At one time or another several letterboxes have appeared across the down. Here is the current stamp in memory of Old Jack.

ONWARD, LETTERBOXERS

To be sung, with determination, to the tune of
"Onward, Christian soldiers"

Onward, letterboxers,
Striding 'cross the Moor,
With our map and compass
Hanging down before.
Thermos in our rucksack,
Lev'nses, lunch and tea,
Kendal Mint Cake, Mars Bars
Well equipped are we.

CHORUS

> Onward, letterboxers,
> Striding 'cross the Moor,
> With our map and compass
> Hanging down before.

Off we go a-hunting,
Filled with hope and glee,
Seeking letterboxes
Hidden carefully.
Check those clues again now,
"Find a lonely tree,
Then go fifty paces,
Bearing one two three".

CHORUS

Here's a likely boulder:
Underneath's a hole
Hid by rocks and heather:
This must be our goal.
Dump our rucksacks down now,
Move the stones aside,
Here's the box to open:
Let's see what's inside.

CHORUS

Use the stamp and inkpad,
Put them back again
Making sure that all is
Safe from wind and rain.
Onward to the next box
Plodding on our way,
Always seeking one more
So we pass the day.

CHORUS

Onward, PENSIONED PLODDER,
NIMROD, MORRIS MAN,
LONE WOLF, DARTMOOR BOUNDER,
KILROY, DESPERATE DAN.
Forward, SODDEN BOGGERS,
PAWS AWHILE, OLD NOG,
DRAMATORIST, STRIDER,
ONE MAN AND HIS DOG.

Onward, letterboxers,
Striding 'cross the Moor,
With our map and compass
Hanging down before.

99

Great Nodden
River Lyd
North Dartmoor

Wheatear

GREAT NODDEN, or Noddon, is perhaps a corruption of North Down. This high rounded hill lies on the very edge of Dartmoor, and is well worth the climb to its summit. The view from here extends Westward well into Cornwall.

The hill is not of granite but of metamorphosed shale. The young Lyd, running between it and Great Links Tor, separates the two types of rock. Granite from the tor and shale from the hill can be easily distinguished in the stream.

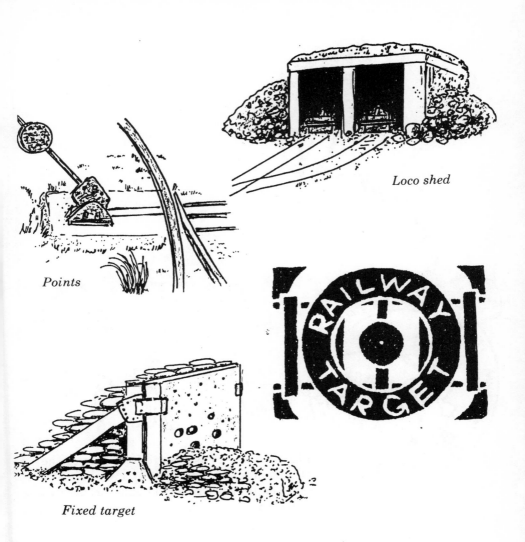

Loco shed

Points

Fixed target

Not far South of Row Tor is a little railway about 200 yards long with a loop at each end. A loco shed contains two target trolleys, each with a rusting motor. The self-propelled trolleys would run backwards or forwards behind a low bank. At the shed end is a hand lever for moving the points, while at the other end the junction is spring loaded so that the target would loop round and return automatically.

The line is no longer in use, but the nearby letterbox lies nevertheless within the Firing Area.

DARTMOOR PONIES

Loughtor Man

PISKIES and PONIES are both part of the Dartmoor scene and here at Laughter Tor (once called more simply Lough Tor) are two letterboxes to remind us of their presence.

Down the hill at Laughter Hole a number of people have attested to seeing a troupe of pixies—and in daylight too. And on neighbouring Bellever Tor poor Tom White journeying home to Postbridge one night from a rendezvous with his sweetheart, was so overcome by a group of whirling pixies that he never again dared go that way after dark.

This fine menhir stands not far to the South of the tor at the head of a double stone row.

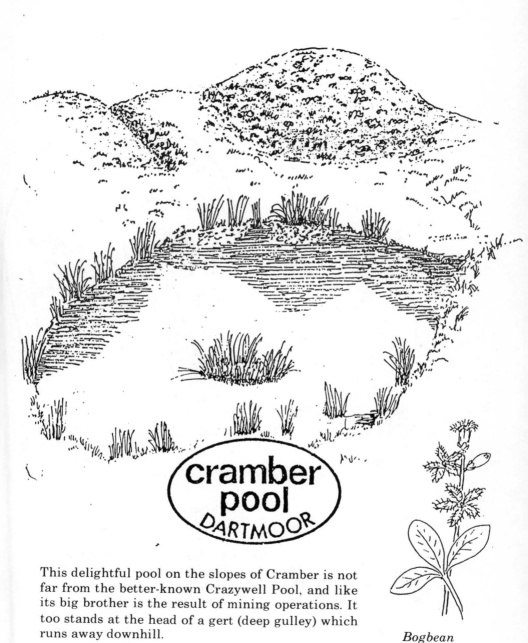

cramber pool DARTMOOR

Bogbean

This delightful pool on the slopes of Cramber is not far from the better-known Crazywell Pool, and like its big brother is the result of mining operations. It too stands at the head of a gert (deep gulley) which runs away downhill.

In Summer spikes of Bogbean pierce the surface and Whortleberries are plentiful nearby.

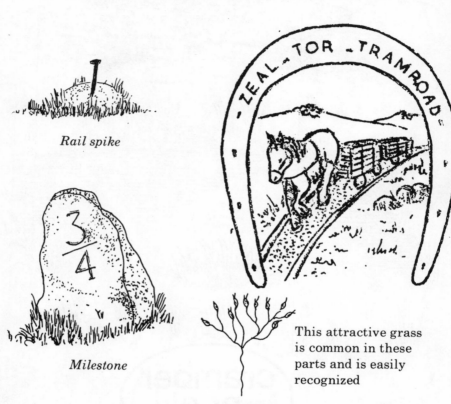

Eastern White Barrow on the Northern horizon

Rail spike

Milestone

This attractive grass is common in these parts and is easily recognized

Wavy Hair-grass

The Zeal Tor Tramway, running South from Redlake, was built in 1847 to carry peat down to works at Shipley Bridge, where naphtha was extracted from it. The wooden rails were fastened to granite sleepers by iron spikes, some of which may still be found.

However the venture did not long prosper. It closed down in 1850.

The milestone stands by the track near Western White Barrow, while the letterbox is further South on Brent Moor.

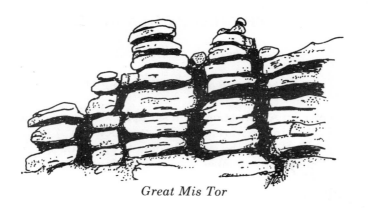

Great Mis Tor

The "Devil's Frying Pan" as it is popularly known, or Mistor Pan as it is named on the map, is one of the best-known ROCK BASINS on Dartmoor. Rock basins are formed when water lies for long periods in shallow troughs on exposed slabs of granite. They are often high on the tors, open to the action of frost which slowly prises out specks of embedded crystals, thus gradually widening and deepening the basin. Any measurement of the annual increase in size would be a fraction of a millimetre.

The largest rock basin on Dartmoor is on Kestor, but this one, which is 3 feet across and about 7 inches deep, is the first to have a historical reference—about 1280. The Perambulation to refix the Forest Bounds in 1609 specifically mentions Mis Tor Pan as a boundary mark.

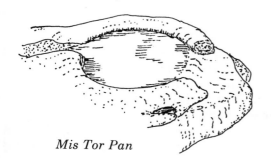

Mis Tor Pan

The Devil's Pan is on the summit of one of the rock piles of Great Mis Tor, but no rock climbing is needed to locate the letterbox.

THE HAPPY STAMPER

Memories of an Australian letterboxer

To be sung to the tune "Waltzing Matilda"

Once an Aussie stampman sat upon a logging stone
Bathed in the warmth of the afternoon sun,
And he sang as he sat and counted up the ones he'd found:
"I'm a happy stamper, o what jolly fun,
98 boxes, 98 boxes,
I'm a happy stamper, o what jolly fun."
And he sang as he sat and counted up the ones he'd found:
"I'm a happy stamper, o what jolly fun."

Up strode a Ranger, hiding 'neath a woolly hat,
Headed on a bearing three two one.
"There's another letterbox underneath the rock
    you're on."
"I'm a happy stamper, o what jolly fun,
98 boxes, 98 boxes,
I'm a happy stamper, o what jolly fun.
There's another letterbox underneath the rock
    I'm on?
I'm a happy stamper, o what jolly fun."

Up leapt the stampman, searched beneath the logging stone,
Found there a canister: mission nearly done.
And he sang as he knelt and stamped up yet another card,
"I'm a happy stamper, o what jolly fun,
99 boxes, 99 boxes,
I'm a happy stamper, o what jolly fun."
And he sang as he knelt and stamped up yet another card,
"I'm a happy stamper, o what jolly fun."

Away went the stampman, hurried off to Princytown,
One more letterbox—his badge would be won;
So he sang as he ran and headed for 'The Feather'd Plume',
"I'm a happy stamper, o what jolly fun,
Nearly got a 100, soon I'll have a 100,
I'm a happy stamper, o what jolly fun."
And he sang as he ran and headed for 'The Feather'd Plume',
"I'm a happy stamper, o what jolly fun."

ICH DIEN

GOAL !

When you find this letterbox you will be in Happy Valley, not a hundred stone-throws from the loneliest pub in England.

You have attained your goal.

You have earned a drink. Go and celebrate.

Pub letterboxes do not really count—but they are very popular!

So overleaf is one more stamp, and one more song.

If letterboxes can be said to have patrons then that is certainly the right word for those who visit this one. On a cold, blustery Winter day the view from the box is warm and comforting.

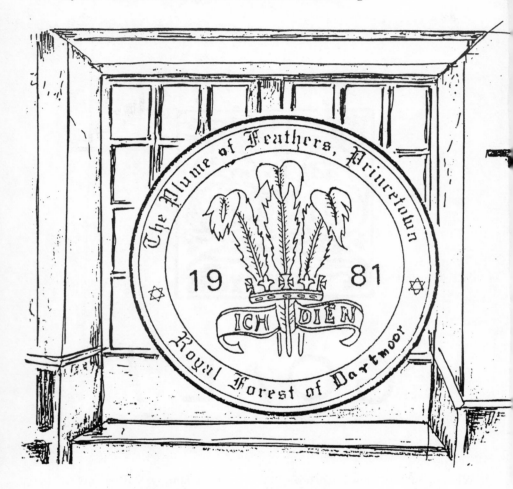

A cheerful welcome awaits you here but if you are short of time beware the clock behind the bar: its hands move in mysterious ways.

A number of other inns on and around Dartmoor have a letterbox. The Plume of Feathers was the first to install one, in 1981.

The building is said to be the oldest in Princetown. Enjoy its comfort while you do a little armchair letterboxing.

SING A SONG OF DARTMOOR

Sing a song of moorpubs,
"The Forest" and "The Tors",
Four and twenty inn-mates
Making for the doors.
When the doors are opened
The ale begins to flow,
For that's the sort of gath'ring place
Where letterboxers go.

Godfrey's in "The Warren House"
Looking for some money,
Anne is in "The Ring o' Bells"
Writing something funny.
John is in "The Tavistock"
Sketching in a book,
When down comes a "Mouse" hound
Who wants to have a look.

TAVISTOCK
INN

WARREN HOUSE INN